Growing Up Gay

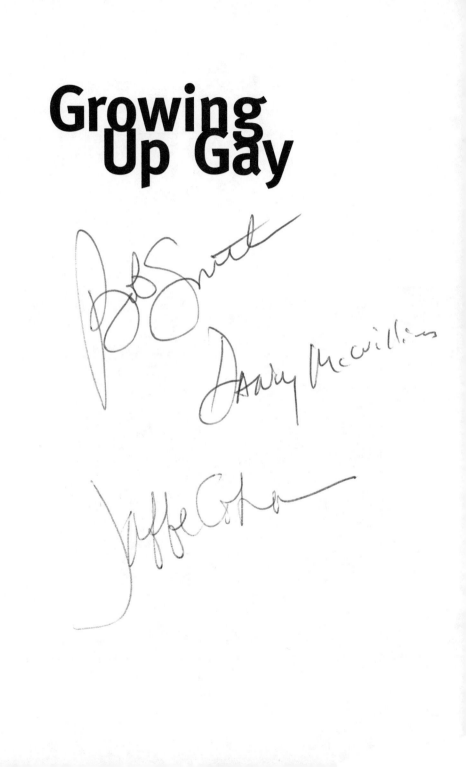

Growing Up Gay

From Left Out to Coming Out

By Funny Gay Males

*Jaffe Cohen, Danny McWilliams,
and Bob Smith*

Illustrations by Michiko Stehrenberger

HYPERION

New York

Library of Congress Cataloging-In-Publication Data
Funny gay males.
Growing up gay : from left out to coming out / by Funny gay males.
p. cm.
ISBN 0-7868-8056-2
1. Gay men—United States. 2. Coming out (Sexual orientation)—United States.
I. Title
HQ76.2.U5F86 1995
305.38´9664—dc20   94–45867 CIP

FIRST EDITION
10 9 8 7 6 5 4 3 2 1

DESIGNED BY JESSICA SHATAN

All interior photographs courtesy of Archive Photos

Acknowledgments

We want to thank our great editor, Rick Kot, who originally suggested the idea for this book and who has been unfailingly patient with our relentless jokes—good, bad, or about Lucy. We also want to thank David Cashion of Hyperion, who tried to keep us on schedule and who never complained once when we would invariably put him on the spot by asking, "Is this funny?" And we also want to thank Michiko Stehrenberger, who did the wonderful illustrations for our book.

We also would like to thank all the people whom we have met over the years who have added to the collective personality of Funny Gay Males. This includes our families and friends, who supplied us with comic materials and have always shown up when we needed to pack an audience. This also includes all the people and venues who gave us a leg up on our careers: The Duplex, Phyllis Schlossberg and The Post Office Cabaret, Donald Montwill and Josie's Juice Joint, William McLaughlin, Stuart Krasnow, The Baltimore Theatre Project, The Red Barn Theatre, The Alice B. Toklas Theatre, The Manhattan Association of Cabarets, Michael Wakefield, Highways, Dean Kogan and The Society Hill Playhouse, The Just For Laughs Festival, Club Cabaret, Barbara Bridges and Robin Tyler, Jonathan Cohen and Howard Stern, Joan Rivers, Milt Tatelman, Michael Zam and Tom Lasley.

And we especially want to thank the large cast of kooks and nutcases whom we've run into over the years. Because even though we've had some unpleasant experiences with a few of them, in the end, they always became a huge source of hilarious private jokes for the three of us.

Table of Contents

Growing Up Gay

Introduction

Did you violate the first commandment of traditional masculinity—thou shalt not covet thy sister's dolls? Was your imaginary friend a hunk? Were you so bored when you watched *Bonanza* that you wanted to burn down the Ponderosa? If you answered "Yes! Yes! Yes!" to the above questions, then there's a strong possibility that you're gay. While as a little boy you may not have known you were queer in the sexual sense, you certainly knew you were different. Let's face it: Society is not in the business of raising homosexuals—we're all brought up to be straight. Even worse, we're all brought up to conform to narrow ideas of what's gender-appropriate in a patriarchal system where Rambo rules and anything less than gung-ho is gung-homo. But fortunately there's always been—for whatever blessed reason—a certain percentage of us who were never meant to be straight.

From very early on we looked at the world differently and, in most cases, we felt absolutely alone. Without knowing it, we were pink triangles in a world made for square pegs. Only much later in life did we discover other members of our tribe and learn—by comparing notes—that we hadn't been the only twelve-year-old boys lipsynching to Aretha Franklin and paying good money to see Lucille Ball in *Mame*. And when we finally did find others like ourselves, we often felt like Bette Davis at the end of *Whatever Happened to Baby Jane?* when she exclaims to her estranged sister, Blanche, "You mean all these years, we could have been friends?!"

Growing Up Gay was inspired by comparing such notes. As three openly gay standup comics working together, we've been mining our memories for years as the source of material for our acts. We've also had the pleasure of performing for and interacting with gay men all over the world, and this is what we've discovered about our collective pasts:

Number One: A gay kid is not just a child who will one day turn into a gay adult. Now that we've come to speak more openly and proudly about our personal histories, we're learning that the gay child—even before the first flush of adolescent hormonal changes, even before he begins socializing with other gay adults—is already sharing likes, dislikes, interests, and outlooks with a worldwide culture of which he's only vaguely aware. In short, we guessed that something was cooking even before we started baking. We knew we were different the first time we noticed Lee Majors was wearing tight pants on *The Big Valley*. We knew we were different the first time we found ourselves daintily shaking a packet of sweetener between our thumb and middle finger just like Aunt Marge. And we knew we were different that first summer we wanted to send a postcard to Johnny saying, "I wish you were here," and the boy in question lived right next door.

Number Two: While this may annoy the politically correct, it must be acknowledged: Many of those stereotypes about gay men are often true, just as many of those adjectives commonly applied to us are not totally inaccurate. We gay boys were—on the average—more "sensitive," "artistic," "animated," and "theatrical" than our peers. "Vivacious," for instance, is a lovely modifier if you happen to be Liza Minnelli, but for a seven-year-old boy, you may just as well use the word "queer," and in most cases, you'd be right on the money. We were—on the average—less likely to want to grow up to be policemen and much more likely to want to play them on TV. Likewise, we started using the word "ambiance" long before anyone else. And if we preferred the company of our cousin Tiffany, it was only because the company of most other young males in this violence-prone society was about as appealing as spending the afternoon with Genghis Khan.

The point is, however, that our differences should have been celebrated and not mocked. Any kid who can recite Thelma Ritter's dialogue from *All About Eve* deserves a lot of credit. In addition, any psychiatrist worth his sea salt will tell you that "masculinity" is a cultural construct, and that every man—gay or straight—has some big old girl inside, just busting to get out. Within every man's psyche there are aspects of a woman. Within every Norman Schwarzkopf, there's a Martha Raye entertaining the troops. Why even Rush Limbaugh has a female side to him—who in his case seems to be spending a lot of time in the kitchen whipping up snacks for his bloated masculine side.

Number Three: On the other hand, gay men are also a lot more complex than straight society cares to imagine. As we become more visible our diversity becomes more apparent. Just as every macho man has a female side, every Carol Channing impersonator has within her girdle a backbone of steel. As hard as it is to believe, even Liberace had a masculine side. There's tremendous variety within the gay community, and to say that every gay man is a drag queen is like saying that, in his heart, every straight man is an Elvis impersonator. Then again, if you saw two men in costumes and one was doing Elvis and the other was doing Priscilla Presley, you could pretty much guess which one was homosexual.

If any generalizations can be made about our gay boyhoods, it's that we were busy synthesizing both so-called male and female values. As boys we went fishing with our dads, but we also could whip up a mean tartar sauce on the side. We collected toads with our friends, but we also used them to cast spells like Endora on *Bewitched*. We were as strong and quick as the other boys even if we were more likely to display these qualities playing Double Dutch with the girls. And now as gay men we're bringing this versatility with us into our personal and professional lives. We lift weights and we lift settees. We're hoping to get into the military and we're hoping to get into the cast of *Miss Saigon*. Last year at the Gay Games—in which many self-described sissies engaged in (and broke records in) competitive sports—that guy spiking the volleyball was also wearing spiked heels later that night.

Number Four: In the final analysis, we gay boys turned out just fine. Without denying that there were difficult times, we still figured out ways to have fun and grow into reasonably happy adults. Moreover, what made us outsiders as kids is often what made us successful as adults. We didn't outgrow things— we just grew into them. All those hours spent rearranging peas and carrots on our plates often evolved into wonderful careers as food stylists. All that eavesdropping on our grandmother's coffee klatches turned into satisfying jobs as family counselors. And, finally, all those lonely afternoons listening to our mothers' records led to ten-week gigs singing Rodgers and Hart at the Carlyle.

And Number Five: This book is not just for homosexuals. You don't have to be gay in order to be queer. Gay kids are not the only children growing up feeling like they'll have to make the best of a world that wasn't intended for them—many straight kids feel the exact same way. Let's face it: Every child thinks he or she is different. Most kids aren't one hundred percent comfortable being harnessed into rigid gender roles, and we all have secrets. We've all been forced to pretend. We're all emerging from a closet of one sort or another. Furthermore, gay adults are not the only ones who find it necessary to venture beyond the rules we were taught as children. You don't have to be a gay boy not to want to play with plastic machine guns, and you don't have to be a gay man to realize that Charlton Heston and the NRA are menaces to a free society.

We're approaching a new millenium. These are the Gay Nineties—a time when society is changing so fast that even the straightest of the straights are discovering that the only sane approach to life is to learn how to wing it. Well, gays have been winging it for centuries—seasoning our lives according to personal taste. Living life as an openly gay individual requires daily acts of self-assertion, which is a strategy that everyone has to learn sooner or later. In order to give of yourself you have to first be yourself.

This book, then, is being written for anyone who's genuinely excited about the advances we're making in identifying who we are—gay and straight—and how we can most ideally relate to one another. In the final analysis, our *real* traditional values are not sexism, racism, and homophobia but tolerance and the desire to live together harmoniously. Speaking as optimists we can see the American creed of fairness being applied to all of us regardless of gender, creed, color, hair color, or shade of lipstick.

• • •

In conclusion, our goal was to create the book we wish we'd had when we were growing up. Although this book is primarily for adults, we authors are very aware of the lonely gay teenager, and so we dedicate *Growing Up Gay* to all the gay youngsters out there who were bred by heterosexuals, raised on junk media, and then put out to pasture in antiseptic malls all across America. Just like you we snuck into bookstores and thumbed through anything that might have the word "gay" or "lesbian" emblazoned within: novels, collections of movie reviews, medical dictionaries, Elton John songbooks, periodicals about women's tennis. Anything! So, hey kid, if that's you crouched in the humor section of B. Dalton Books, get up and brush the dust off your knees. Read this book before starting out. We wrote it for you and any other gay kid who had to grow up thinking he was the only one.

Born to Be Wilde:
From Conception Through Kindergarten

> "There is what one might call
> a natural homosexuality
> in the animal kingdom."
>
> —*On Life and Living,* Konrad Lorenz,
> Nobel Prize–winner for his work in animal behavior

Chapter 1

Origins of the Species

Before we delve into our collective memories we want to deal briefly with the endlessly controversial question, "Where do gay children come from?" Is it nature? Is it nurture? If straight kids are found in the cabbage patch, are gay kids discovered under the arugula? Or are we gay kids simply delivered by pink flamingos? There are so many theories about what causes homosexuality that first we might need to debunk a few ridiculous myths—before creating a few new ones of our own.

1. Homosexuality is not caused by drinking strawberry-flavored milk. Although many gay men remember being the only ones in their family who would drink this weird concoction, the odds are that the correlation is coincidental rather than causal. Similarly, homosexuality is not caused by a particular brand of cookies, fruitcake, or—in Jewish families—your mother's favorite marble cake. Nei-

ther is homosexuality caused by banana daiquiris or any
other alcoholic beverage served with a paper umbrella.

2. Homosexuality is not caused by your parents' having
watched a campy TV show on the night you were con-
ceived. If this were the case, then a glut of gay boys would
have been born nine months after the airing of Lucy's fabulous "Vitameatavegimin" episode. Similarly, homosexuality
is not caused by what happened to be playing most often on
TV while you were crawling around the living room. In
other words, Virginia Graham's *Girl Talk* did not cause us
to be gay: It merely gave us ideas for Halloween costumes
later on in life.

3. Homosexuality has nothing to do with how the baby is
carried in the womb. While there may be some truth to the
old wives' tales about girls being carried low and wide and
boys being carried high and up front, it is highly unlikely
that a gay boy would be carried under the arm like a
clutch, or that a baby lesbian would sit on her mother's
back like a fanny pack.

4. Homosexuality is not
caused by that old buga-
boo—a domineering
mother and a distant
father. For one thing,
if this hypothesis
were true, every male
child born since the
Industrial Rev-
olution, when
fathers began

working away from home, would have turned out gay. In addition, if a domineering mother could turn a male homosexual, what would keep her from wrecking her havoc on every male she came in contact with—her brothers, her husband? Why, we ourselves have seen some mothers so domineering that even the postman delivering the mail would suddenly turn gay just by walking up the driveway. We authors feel that this theory is absolutely ridiculous and no doubt devised by reactionaries to suppress women by giving them one more thing to feel guilty about. To these people we would like to point out that the ultimate distant father was God—think of the consequences.

5. And, finally, homosexuality is not caused by an overly strong and affectionate bond between mother and son. While gay men do often manifest a peculiar form of the Oedipal conflict summed up by the statement "We'd like to kill our fathers and go shopping with our mothers," we authors doubt that this actually caused us to be gay. It's really a question of what came first, the chicken Florentine or the eggs Benedict? Perhaps we weren't gay because our mothers loved us, but, rather, our mothers loved us because we often complimented them and shared their taste in old movies. I mean, who else but a gay boy would coo to his beloved mother, "Mommy, you look just like Donna Reed"?

In short, we're much more likely to agree with current thinking that homosexuality is biological in nature—although we're not overly impressed with the research so far. Recently we've been following the findings of a Dr. Simon Levay, who attempted to prove that the hypothalamuses of gay men were smaller than those of straight men. While Dr. Levay's studies have yet to be corroborated, further research seems to point out that gay men, on the average, also have a far greater ability to pronounce the word "hypothalamus."

Obviously, more research must be done, because gay men's brains are definitely different from those of straights. What else but a twisted cortical structure could account for all those boys who think that Steven Seagal is an actor? What else but a structural defect in the nervous system could be responsible for the idea that working on cars is a form of relaxation? What else but a radically damaged body chemistry could have produced a Jesse Helms? An Andrew Dice Clay? The answer, we feel, must lie in our genes, and we're fairly certain that when more research is completed, we'll see that although gay men and straight men both have the same number of X and Y chromosomes—ours are drawn more stylishly.

In conclusion, we approve of this new emphasis on biology, for, if nothing else, it will disprove the ridiculous notion we somehow chose to be gay in order to embarrass our families. Also, we're looking forward to an enlightened era when mothers will be able to tell in advance that they are carrying a gay baby and thus take steps to make that baby feel welcome by listening to the latest dance music and by strolling through trendy neighborhoods during pregnancy. Which brings up an obvious question: If a fetus is gay, would the expectant mother of a gay boy be seized by sudden cravings for something a little more elegant than the traditional sardines? How about lobster thermidor or linguini with pesto?

A far more fascinating question is, "If being gay is biologically determined, are the different species of gay men biologically determined as well?" Let us not forget that, despite a recent trend for all gay men to achieve the same body type at the gym, our community is extremely diverse. One gene does not fit all. If it were still possible, for instance, to stand Truman Capote between Bob and Rod Jackson-Paris, we would seem to be looking at two different breeds.

With this idea in mind we authors have prepared brief descriptions of the six major types of gay men as we've seen them evolve thus far. Before we proceed, we should probably warn you that we will be using the term "queen." Although some people may find this word offensive or dated, we find this word far too useful to ban it from our vocabulary. It's important to remember, however, that the word "queen" is neither pejorative nor necessarily complimentary. We believe it to be a neutral term meaning nothing more than the word "guy" might mean to a straight man, as in the sentence, "Who does that queen think she is?" Also, when the word "queen" is preceded by a modifier, it takes on a specific meaning—and one gay culture could probably not survive without—that of "fan" or "buff," as in the sentence, "Warren is such an opera queen!" With this in mind, if you happen to overhear a conversation and catch the term "muscle queen," you will realize that the speaker is referring to a gay man who works out at the gym— and not Queen Elizabeth on steroids bench pressing 260.

In any event, we believe the following six types of "queens" to be genetically determined, with different roots in the far distant pasts and distinct paths of historical development. In essence, they constitute the six basic gay subsets of Homo sapiens:

1. Homo sashaypiens. Also known as the common drag queen. (Although in our politically correct age, these men often prefer to be called "People of Hair Color.") Current thinking now places the dawn of Homo sashaypiens as far back as one million BC—Before Chanel—when one of these hardy anthropoids was first able to stand upright in pumps. While Homo sashaypiens did not invent the wheel, they certainly did invent the heel. Later in its evolution, during the Rhinestone Age, Homo sashaypiens moved out of the forests and into the cities, where it traveled in small bands gathering accessories. Nowadays, this species has tended to cluster in urban centers such as the East Village, or Atlantic City, New Jersey, or anyplace where men can forage for women's shoes size twelve and up.

Biologically the Homo sashaypien is a breed apart, and recent studies on the anatomy of these multifaceted creatures have yielded interesting results. While still in the womb, embryonic drag queens instinctively drape the umbilical cords across their shoulders in preparation for handling feather boas later in life. In many cases these fetuses have displayed the amazing ability to tuck—in other words, when a sonogram is taken, they can make their natural genitalia all but disappear.

As infants, Homo sashaypiens make intricate motions with their mouths, which only recently have been recognized as early attempts to lipsynch. Many mothers of this breed will discover that, while other toddlers are learning to talk, this child will just sit in front of the TV and move his lips. The first major display of Homo sashaypien plumage generally occurs on their favorite holiday, Halloween. Foregoing the usual ghosts, goblins, and superheroes, baby drag queens are often seen thumbing through *Vogue* and *Hollywood Confidential* for costume ideas. It would not be unusual, for instance, to see a young Homo sashaypien strutting from door to door dressed as Tallulah Bankhead.

2. *Homo cabaretpiens*. Also known as "chorus boys," "gypsies," and "show queens." Homo cabaretpiens' contribution to culture is legendary and diverse. Evidence is now surfacing that indicates that Homo cabaretpiens were putting on shows as far back as the Ice Age Capades, although it is widely believed that they had to wait for the climate to change before inventing summer stock. In addition to developing theater back in ancient Greece, show queens can also be credited with starting the cult of the actor/waiter, whereby struggling performers hoping for parts in the chorus of *Oedi-*

pus Rex had to support themselves slinging hash at The Parthenon Diner.

Nowadays, the typical Homo cabaretpien is nostalgic not only for his own childhood but for his mother's childhood as well, and he can most often be sighted in a gathering around a piano, holding margaritas in both hands and singing songs that would otherwise be extinct. He also tends to be most fond of obscure Broadway musicals that—although he would argue otherwise—closed quickly and for very good reasons. Unlike his drag queen cousin, the Homo cabaretpien doesn't want to be a glamourous woman—he merely wants to dance behind them, write songs for them, spread gossip about them, and do their hair.

Homo cabaretpiens also have strong religious natures. They tend to worship the Mother Goddess in all her forms, from the Virgin Mary to Mary Pickford to Mary Tyler Moore. They are particularly drawn to those icons who are so famous that they can be referred to by only one name—or what we call mononyms—such as Judy, Lucy, Barbra, Joan (Crawford and Rivers), and Marilyn (Monroe, but not Quayle). Many show queens also swoon over the oeuvres of character actresses whose names would mean nothing to the average man on the street. On the other hand, male movie stars mean almost nothing to Homo cabaretpiens, unless they were strongly rumored to have been gay—Sal Mineo, Montgomery Clift, and James Dean come to mind. It would be unusual, however, to hear a show queen discussing the careers of Glenn Ford or Lee Marvin.

A subgenre of the Homo cabaretpien is the Homo critic, who also builds his nest in the world of show business, but has evolved into a spiteful creature with his nose in the air who delights in ripping apart any performer who's achieved a modicum of success. These are the vultures who can savagely pick apart Bette Midler's latest concert three months before she actually steps on stage. And these are the critics who, after visiting Seaworld, are likely to sniff, "Those dolphins just swam through their parts. Where was the emotion?"

3. *Homo drapeiens.* Also known as the "Decorator," the "Window Dresser," and the "Designer." Homo drapeiens have been with us for over a million years, ever since one of them first stood upright in order to hang curtains and straighten a frame around a cave painting. Other early achievements include the early domestication of the wild yorkie and the construction of Stonehenge, which experts now believe was built as a coffee table for the gods. These men have one goal in life: to make the world more beautiful, which they express in the philosophy, "Throw pillows, not stones."

Homo drapeiens are often very vain. They are expert poseurs— knowing just how far they can suck in their cheeks to give their faces bone structure—and even their driver's license pictures are often taken over their shoulders. They also frequently dye their hair blond and tell you that the sun did it, even while you're thinking to yourself, *Where? On Mercury?* Also, once Homo drapeiens discover a trend they are likely to carry it to extremes. These are the men prone to installing track lighting in their refrigerators. They are also masters of artifice, and they pride themselves on accomplishing more with less. The results, however, are sometimes disastrous. We know of one young Homo drapeien living in Hell's Kitchen who figured out a way of using mirrors to make his studio apartment look like a twelve-room apartment on Central Park West. Unfortunately, when the sunlight came in his sofa went up in flames.

4. *Homo in-shapeiens.* Also known as "muscle queens," "gym boys," and "get a load of her." In ancient as well as modern times, the hardy Homo in-shapeien has been worshipped as gods. Apparently, they have been around since the dawn of man, when the first Cro-Magnon aspired to achieve a Neanderthal physique. And while the rest of mankind was going through the Bronze Age, they were going through The Bronzer Age—a period during which self-tanning cream was invented.

Biologically this species is definitely a breed apart. Their bodies are so hard and ruddy that some scientists would classify them as having exoskeletons, putting them in the Crustacean family along with Maine lobsters. In terms of body fat, Homo inshapeians rarely exceed 2 percent—the level of skimmed milk—and they tend to spend so much time at the gym that they become disoriented in rooms that are not mirrored from floor to ceiling.

Their language skills are generally limited to grunted expressions like "Big arms!" "Yeah!" and "Uggh." Their self-involvement generally leaves little time for attention to other species, and so when they refer to a "problem area" they are usually talking about a minute bulge on their waistlines and not, for instance, Bosnia. It should also be pointed out that, strictly speaking, one doesn't need to be gay in order to be a Homo in-shapeien. Sylvester Stallone, Arnold Schwarzenegger, and Joe Piscopo—whether they know it or not—are definitely muscle queens.

5. *Homo suedepiens*. Also known as the "leather man," or just plain "sir." Of all the species of homosexuals, Homo suedepien has changed the least since prehistoric times. In terms of fashion, his idea of a Halston is still a Holstein. Homo suedepiens are also credited with having invented the harness during the Mesolithic period—not for agricultural purposes, as previously thought, but as a trendy outfit. It was also during this period that they came upon the notion of using metal rings for clothing—the idea being, "If it looked good through the bull's nose, it'll look good on me."

Nowadays many Homo suedepiens are also partial to body piercing. They are often decorated with enough earrings through each ear to hang shower curtains. The more practical of this group hang their house keys, guest towels, and/or a Phillips screwdriver on any appendage that sticks out far enough to install a hook. In short, the typical Homo suedepien doesn't feel fully dressed unless he's sporting enough leather and chrome to resemble the front end of a Buick, and he can often be seen thumbing through Sears auto repair catalogues looking for ideas on accessories.

In terms of mating habits, the Homo suedepien's taste in men has been unaffected by any advance in civilization since Paleolithic times: They still like them big and hairy, with thick brows. In terms of typical relationships, they run toward the—how shall we say—hierarchical. One can safely assume that when a leather queen refers to his "daddy" that he's not talking about the man who paid for his Bar Mitzvah and/or cosigned his student loan.

6. *Homo scrapeiens*. The "politically correct activist" is always looking for a noble fight against authority. Although scrappy by nature, the Homo scrapiens almost died out in prehistoric times because they were so sensitive to the rights of mastodons that they refused to wear fur. Until recent times the most obvious achievements of the Homo scrapeiens occurred during the American war for independence, when they not only organized the Boston Tea Party but the Boston tea dance immediately following the "zap"—in which prizes were given out for the best Indian costumes.

In modern times the hardy Homo scrapeiens were most visible during the heyday of organizations such as ACT UP and Queer Nation, when one could barely cross a main boulevard without tripping over an activist sitting in the middle of the street and blocking traffic. It was during this period that Homo scrapeiens contributed the word "homophobic" to our vocabulary. This term quickly spread to refer to any situation that caused gay men the least discomfort. If our MasterCard bill was too high, the company was homophobic; if our scrambled eggs were served dry, the waitress was homophobic; if we got turned down for a date on a Saturday night, it was because the guy we lusted after was an internalized homophobic.

Nowadays Queer Nation is gone, but its fashion statement remains. As of this writing, the typical Homo scrapeien is more noted for his clothing than his political beliefs. Typically his

black leather jacket is covered with so many buttons and pink triangles that he has developed back problems from all the extra weight. He also prefers to buy jeans so ripped and slashed that he looks as if he ran into Freddy Krueger on his way out of the store. Rebelling against the blow-dried, moustachioed look of the seventies, the trendy nineties Homo scrapeien has developed a bald-headed, goateed look—which just goes to prove that no matter the decade, "Hair today, clone tomorrow."

Finally, in concluding this chapter on natural gay types, we should also point out that we gay men are very versatile by nature, and that it would be rare to find a pure breed of any one category. We are always mixing and matching. Homo drapeiens, for instance, often aspire to be Homo in-shapeiens, and they very often do develop muscular bodies, which they then wear like sweaters bought from Bloomingdale's. Also Homo sashaypiens are very often Homo scrapeiens, as we've learned from the history of the Stonewall riots. In addition, the average drag queen is almost by definition a show queen—unless he wants to spend his whole life dressed up as his boring Aunt Beatrice. And even the toughest-looking Homo suedepien is often a Homo cabaretpien at heart and can sometimes be seen rusting his nipple rings crying over Judy's performance in *Meet Me in St. Louis*. In short, gay men—like all God's creatures—come in all sizes and shapes. If variety is the spice of life, then gay men are nothing less than the parsley, sage, rosemary, and thyme that makes the melting pot just a little more savory.

Chapter 2

Am I Blue?

t's a boy!!!

With those few words our gender was announced—and with this brief sentence went an unstated set of expectations and obligations as to our future behavior. From this point on parents, siblings, and the whole rest of society did their best to reinforce what was considered properly masculine. Now, none of these ploys were particularly successful with little gay boys, and we soon became anxiously aware that we were being forced to play roles for which we were ill suited. As a result of this we learned to hide any behavior that wasn't considered manly, and for many of us masculinity became *mask*ulinity.

As adults we can look back in annoyance at what was done to us in our early years—and in this spirit of sweet revenge we offer the following critiques of the absurd ways that society tried to butch us up.

1. They wrapped us in blue blankets. Even before we left the delivery room we were color-coded according to sex—

blue for boys and pink for girls—even though only the most primitive thinking would conclude that the limitless possibilities for sexual identity could be reduced to two colors. Why, most gay men know that you can't limit even the possibilities for bathroom wallpaper to 500. If nothing else there should have been different shades of blue for different types of boys. A gay boy headed for a career in show business might have been better off swathed in powder blue, whereas a gay boy headed for the military might have been better off in navy. And if our nervous mothers thought that this color-coding might actually promote masculine behavior, there's evidence that this mistaken perception can backfire. Baby Quentin Crisp, for instance, was no doubt also wrapped in a blue blanket, which did nothing for him later in life but influence his choice in hair color.

In fact the only person who might have benefited from this binary system was the young drag queen. Later in life the Homo sashaypien spends hundreds of dollars for the wig, makeup, and gown that make him indistinguishable from the opposite sex. Ironically, as a newborn all he had to do was swathe himself in an inexpensive pink blanket and he would have achieved the same illusion.

2. *They dressed us in appropriate male attire.* After we left the hospital, our parents invested huge sums of money dressing us in baby-sized football jerseys, Western wear, military camouflage, etc. For those parents who might still believe that the proper butch clothing is insurance against their boys' turning out queer, we offer three words to disprove your theory—The Village People.

3. *They spoke to us in a rugged tone of voice.* Recent studies on young mothers indicate that they use very different tones of voice when speaking to young boys than they do to girls. Whereas baby girls are often coddled and cooed to in soprano voices that would make Beverly Sills wince, adults often imitate John Wayne when talking to "little men." Deep voices, however, are not synonymous with male heterosexuality. Why, just look at Suzanne Pleshette. This picture of female elegance has a voice so gravelly one could black out the picture on the TV screen and swear that Bob Newhart was married to Harvey Fierstein. And there are certainly many gay men who don't mince when they enunciate. For instance, Jeff Stryker, the deep-throated porn star, is obviously gay as a goose, and yet speaks in a voice that would make Bea Arthur sound like Shirley Temple. In fact, Jeff Stryker's speech patterns are so unique that we can only assume that he learned them as a child, maybe even from his mother. A career persona may have been born the first time Mrs. Stryker snarled to him at dinnertime in a basso profundo voice, "You like my meat loaf, don'cha? Then eat the whole thing! You know you want it."

4. They sang us lullabies with sexist lyrics. How many of us remember that egregious little song that was drummed into our heads as infants:

> *Sugar and spice and everything nice—*
> *That's what little girls are made of.*
> *Toads and snails and puppy dog tails—*
> *That's what little boys are made of.*

We beg to differ. If one must stereotype, we gay boys would have much preferred being compared to cinnamon or paprika rather than some slimy amphibian or the rear end of a hound. Therefore we offer this alternative rhyme:

Sensible heels and pottery wheels—
That's what queer girls are made of.
Glitter and brie and gay repartee—
That's what queer boys are made of.

Budding show queens probably tired especially quickly of their mothers' limited repertoire of lullabies. Let's face it, "Rock-a-bye Baby on the Treetop" didn't exactly have us humming in our bassinets. If only our mothers had known better and bought a Sondheim songbook. Wouldn't we have loved to have heard our moms crooning "Rose's Turn" from *Gypsy*?

4. They decorated our nurseries in less than festive colors. Once again there was usually a world of difference between how a parent prepared the room for a baby boy or girl. Whereas little girls tended to be surrounded by fairy princesses and Sleeping Beauty's castle, we little boys were often dumped into rooms desecrated by sports, military, and Western motifs. No wonder we cried day and night. It was bad enough that they dared to decorate our rooms without getting our opinions, but then they inflicted a Hopalong Cassidy bedspread on us. If they really wanted to make us feel at home they might have ripped down those Knicks posters and wallpapered our rooms using the covers of old *Playbills*. And if all else failed, they might have lured us to sleep using a disco ball as a nightlight.

5. They threw balls at us and just took it for granted we would catch them. Why was it assumed that, just by virtue of our having penises we had an innate ability to throw and catch balls? The two were not connected. Nor can it be said that playing sports inherently builds character, for there have been many recent news stories to back us up on that account. We were particularly annoyed at that traditional taunt,

"You throw like a girl!!" which was directed at any boy who showed less athletic ability than Willie Mays. It was horrible insults like these that caused many of us to spend our childhoods trying to run away from home plate.

6. They gave us really tough-sounding names.

In an effort to forge masculine identities, some parents—in displays of wishful thinking—often chose overly butch names for us. Well, guess what? If they named us Brick, it didn't ensure that we'd turn out to be rugged construction workers: We could have just as easily ended up a tortured homosexual in a Tennessee Williams play. This principle also holds true for our sisters: If a girl was named Daisy, it didn't mean that she'd grow up into a dainty little flower—she might have blossomed into an outdoorsy type who enjoyed lugging around hundred-pound bales of peat moss.

In conclusion, the naming of any child—gay or straight—is a complex issue, and we can offer but one rule of thumb: As a parent, try to imagine that name being called out the first day of school, and if there is the remotest possibility of laughter, pick something else. And we don't want to hear that an unusual name builds character. Character is formed from observing parental behavior; it is not a muscle built up from having to carry the burden of being named Silas or Wendall. We firmly believe that parents should be severely limited as to how they label their offspring. Forsythia and Marsden should not be allowed! In fact, we believe that, by law, every birth certificate should have the following provision that has to be signed before the document is issued: Warning: Picking a name for your child is not an opportunity for you to express your creativity. If you feel the need to be artistic, take a pottery class, or write haiku.

Chapter 3

The Gay
Baby Book

Another common tradition in straight culture is to keep a "baby book." The idea behind this is to commemorate the milestones in a child's life. Many gay men look back on our parents' sentimental prehistoric record-keeping with a combination of wistfulness and dismay. Since many of our parents were usually in denial about our true natures, we tend not to trust their judgments of the real accomplishments in our lives. Who cares when we first ate solid food? It was our first champagne brunch that really changed our lives.

As gay men, we often feel that our lives began not when we emerged from the womb but when we emerged from the closet. Our baby book, therefore, would have to include not just our first steps but our first steps as a gay man in a gay culture: our first crush; our first time at a dance club; the first time we saw Barbra Streisand. Life is nothing but a series of first steps, so in the spirit of recognizing that journey, we offer the following: the first baby book that not only lists milestones from infancy but carries us on through our entire lives as gay men.

The Gay Baby Book

Weight at birth: 7 pounds, 4 ounces
Weight upon coming out of the closet: 143 pounds, 6 percent body fat
Hair color at birth: Brown
Hair color upon coming out of the closet: Platinum
Eye color at birth: Brown
Eye color upon coming out of the closet: Azure (contact lenses)

~ Milestones ~

The first time you ever…

Smiled _____

Laughed _____

Pretended to laugh _____

Were laughed at _____

Made people laugh at a party _____

Got the last laugh _____

Went out _____

Came out _____

Came out to your family _____

Came out at work _____

Ran out of people to come out to_____

Went out in a stroller _____

Went out of your mind _____

Had to go on the wagon _____

Went on a trip _____

Tripped on Ecstasy _____

Recognized your name _____

Recognized a celebrity's name_____

Recognized that a favorite celebrity was gay___

Recognized your parents' faces _____

Recognized your parents'
limitations _____

Discovered your hands _____

Discovered your problem area _____

Discovered your middle finger _____

Gave someone your middle finger _____

Sat up_____

Did sit-ups _____

Crawled _____

Came crawling back to Broadway _____

Stood up _____

Got stood up _____

Stood up for your rights _____

Took your first step _____

Did the Stairmaster _____

Went two-stepping _____

Joined a twelve-step

program _____

Walked across the room _____

Walked out in a huff _____

Heard the song *These Boots are Made for
   Walking* _____

Ran _____

Runway modeled _____

Vogued _____

Got mad _____

Got mad and organized a demonstration _____

Cried _____

Was told big boys don't cry _____

Cried while watching *Dark Victory* _____

Cried for Argentina _____

Napped _____

Napped before The White Party _____

Slept through the night _____

Stayed for breakfast _____

Ate solid food _____

Served solid food _____

Complained about the tip _____

Grabbed something _____

Threw something _____

Threw something like a girl _____

Threw a temper tantrum _____

Had a hissy fit _____

Spilled milk _____

Spilled the beans _____

Spilled a frozen margarita _____

Raised your head _____

Raised one eyebrow _____

Learned your phone number _____

Slipped someone your phone number _____

Waited for him to call _____

Called the party line _____

Played with a toy boat _____

Went on a cruise _____

Cruised _____

Cruised Tom Cruise _____

Drank from a bottle _____
Battled with the bottle _____

Waved bye-bye _____
Waved bye-bye and thought good riddance _____

Had your first haircut _____
Hated your hair _____
Worried about baldness _____
Shaved your head _____

Said your first word _____
Had the last word _____
Had your first scathingly brilliant idea _____

Learned your numbers _____

Learned you were a number _____

Clapped your hands _____

Heard Lauren Bacall in *Applause* _____

Tied your shoes _____

Tied up your boyfriend _____

Dressed yourself _____

Accessorized _____

Overdressed yourself _____

First birthday gift _____

What you exchanged it for _____

Played house _____

Moved out of the house _____

Browsed through *Architectural Digest* _____

Drove a toy car _____

Made out in a car _____

Bought a Volvo station wagon for your boyfriend
and dogs _____

~

As we said earlier, gay men come in six different categories, so their baby books would be filled out differently. In the chart below we've speculated on the milestones of the different gay types.

	Homo sashaypien	Homo cabaretpien	Homo drapeien	Homo in-shapeien	Homo suedepien	Homo scrapeien
FIRST COMPLETE SENTENCE	"Is my wig on straight?"	"It's Liza with a z."	I see a big picture window right there."	(Not applicable. Never completes a sentence.)	"Take those two big *bleep bleeps*."	"I'm here. I'm queer. Get used to it."
FIRST PAIR OF SHOES	Pumps	Tap shoes	Tassel loafers	Cross-training Nikes	Army boots	Doc Martens
FAVORITE DOLL	Barbie	Michael Jackson	Forget Barbie. Just give me her dream house.	Masters of the Universe	Ken with pierced ear	Bella Abzug talking action figure
FAVORITE SHOW	*Dynasty*, for Joan Collins's wardrobe	*The Judy Garland Show*	*Martha Stewart Living*	The Soloflex infomercial	*Make Room for Daddy*	*Meet the Press*

And, of course, there will come that moment—we knew it would happen sooner or later—when your baby is no longer a baby. For a gay child, it may be the moment when he starts looking out into the world to make new friends and follows the tried-and-true method of taking out a personal ad:

GWB. Fourteen months. Twenty-three inches tall. Looking for that special Mr. Bubble to share my playpen in a serious long-term relationship. Me? I'm into napping, long crawls on weekends, and intimate Gerber food dinners. I'm in recovery from a recent addiction to baby powder. I'd be in a twelve-step program but I don't know how to walk yet—but I am completely clean now—in fact I've just been changed. You, on the other hand, must be slightly older, toilet trained, own your own stroller. Please no baby fats or fems. If you know your ABC's and can read this ad, I may be the baby for you!!

Chapter 4

Gays 'n Dolls

We are now entering the next phase of our development. This period covers the years one through five, when our main job was to stay home with Mommy and play with our toys. Considering the reputation that gay men have for frivolity, it might be assumed that this was a particularly delightful time for us. Not so. The truth is that during these preschool years the toys we most wanted were the toys most likely to be off-limits. In short, what most of us remember from this time was playing with our Tonka trucks—while our fingers fairly itched for that Skipper doll.

Now why, exactly, were dolls so attractive to us? Consider this: How many of us remember watching our fathers going off to work when it was still dark, freezing cold in winter and unbearably hot in summer, and thinking to ourselves, "Nah, I don't want to do *that*!" Then we'd watch our mothers taking their time getting up, throwing in a load of wash, and then yakking on the phone to their friends. "Yeah, *that's* what I want to be when I get older!" we said to ourselves. The simple fact of the matter is that many of us identified with our mothers' lives, and so the toys we most wanted were those that would have allowed us to practice our nurturing, homemaking, and beauty skills.

For so many of us, the first memory of being in the closet was literally sneaking in there with our sister's EZ Bake oven. The thrill of cooking little cakes and cookies with the heat of a light bulb was for many gay boys a forbidden pleasure that we couldn't resist. We loved this toy so much that, to this very day, you can probably still find gay men on Fire Island trying to brown roasts with flashlights.

The ultimate forbidden pleasure, though, was Barbie. Aaah, Barbie! That pert nose. Those pointy feet. That distinctive smell of plastic. There isn't a gay man alive who as a child didn't secretly pile Barbie's hair on top of her head to make her look just like Bernadette Peters. Our parents did what they could to stop us, but we were drawn to Barbie like a moth to a flame. One gay man we know remembers that his mother actually caught him in the act, ran to the store, and bought him a Masters of the Universe doll instead. When he was presented with this new toy his mother begged him, "Now, honey, I don't want you playing with Barbie. I want you to play with this blond, rippling, muscular He-Man." Our friend now realizes that this was probably the best idea his mother ever had.

There was Ken, of course. He was a male doll, and we were allowed to play with him, but he wasn't nearly as glamourous as Barbie. Yet there was always something intriguingly ambiguous about Barbie's so-called boyfriend. For one thing, Ken was obviously subsidiary, a mere accessory, in Barbie's universe—one of the few times in our childhoods when we witnessed the overturning of patriarchal ranking. Ken had no job, no genitals, and very few male friends. He also seemed happiest hanging out with the girls, and he never complained when we slipped him into Barbie's old blouses. In short, Ken was our first exposure to what we would later recognize as "a bottom." Then in the nineties someone actually came up with the idea for "Magic Earring Ken," who looked like a young Rip Taylor with his poufy hair and shiny shirts. He seemed less like Barbie's boyfriend than a decorator who was panting to redo her dream house.

Now, G.I. Joe was a different story altogether. At some point in the sixties it became acceptable for boys to have a doll as long as he'd been trained as a mercenary killer. G.I. Joe was the rugged top man of our childhoods. Unfortunately there were two main problems with him: His standard-issue clothes were all one color, and all his accessories were instruments of death. Very cleverly—and privately—we began mixing and matching with items from Barbie's wardrobe. Wearing G. I. Joe's uniform, Barbie looked like one of the Andrews sisters, while the cross-dressing G.I. Joe's favorite form of camouflage became oversized sunglasses and a scarf.

"Mixing and matching" in many ways became the story of our childhoods. We quickly learned to take conventional toys and use them in ways that suited our imaginations, soon putting our queer spin on everything we touched. Our tree houses had breakfast nooks. When we played with our toy cars we pretended to pick up handsome hitchhikers. Our sand castles looked like San Simeon, and our snowmen were so handsome that after they were built, *we* would melt.

Our favorite store-bought toys were, nevertheless, gender-neutral items to which we could apply our own creative slant. Thus some of our favorite playthings were:

1. *Silly Putty:* The best thing about Silly Putty was that you could use it to copy pictures out of comic books and magazines and then distort the duplicate picture by stretching the putty this way and that. Future beauticians could practice giving Barbra Streisand a smaller nose. Future muscle boys could take pictures of Pee-Wee Herman and pull out his shoulders to make him look more like Dolph Lundgren.

2. *Slinkies:* For some reason we always delighted in how this thing could flip-flop down the stairs. Like us, a slinkie could bend over backward and still always land on its feet. There was also something almost sensual about the way it could bulge out and then resume its natural shape. Maybe it reminded us of Marilyn Monroe in *Some Like It Hot.*

3. *Aquariums:* Fish tanks were usually one of the few items that we were allowed to decorate to our hearts' content. Colored gravel and underwater knickknacks were relatively cheap, and no matter how garishly we furnished, the guppies never seemed to mind. Also, when nobody was looking, we could pretend Barbie was Esther Williams in our very own MGM musicals.

4. *Indian outfits:* As misfits we often identified with other victims of oppression. Pretending to be an Indian had several other advantages: We got to dress up like Pocahontas, and we also got to choreograph delightful little rain dances—often to the score of *Annie Get Your Gun.*

5. *Toy telephones:* Here was a real chance to imitate our

moms doing the one thing they probably did best—tucking the phone under their ears, yakking incessantly, and still managing to do all the housework. As grown-ups, gay men still continue our love affair with the "Don Ameche," and to say that another gay man "gives good phone" is the highest of compliments.

6. Train sets: For some reason many gay men found toy trains more appealing than toy cars. Cars meant being stuck in a crammed space with nobody but your family, whereas trains offered that perennial gay delight—the chance to meet interesting strangers. In any event, a train set always gave us the opportunity to pretend that we were from the wrong side of the tracks, or simply to hum the "Trolley Song" to our hearts' content.

7. Chemistry sets: These often provided us with a desperately needed sense of omnipotence. If we were angry, we could pretend to be mixing up poison for our older brothers. If we were feeling noble, we could be finding a cure for our grandmothers' arthritis. Once again, if we had known then what we know now, we might have gotten a head start and developed our own line of skin-care products.

8. Stethoscopes: Doctor paraphernalia was always a favorite for gay kids because it gave us an opportunity to, well, play doctor. We usually had our eyes on treating little Joey, but if Bertha insisted on playing doctor with us as well, we just scheduled a consultation and gave her advice on plastic surgery.

However attached we are to the toys of our youth, we'd love to see a time when manufacturers start producing games and toys specifically designed for gay and lesbian children. Imagine: Chatty Cathy dolls that were designed to reproduce only the most

GAYS 'N DOLLS   43

banal heterosexist comments could be revived to sound more like, say, Elaine Stritch, and she could growl, "Here's to the ladies who lunch" every time we pull her string. In fact, an enterprising toy company might even consider coming out with a whole new line of gay talking dolls for children of all ages, such as:

1. Larry the Leatherman, for ages forty and up: Comes with hair on his back that you can style with a pet-grooming brush. When you pull his nipple ring, he grunts, "Hold your head still while I bleep-bleep your bleepin' face."

2. Peter Pee-shy, for older boys: Betsy Wetsy's younger brother, Peter can only wet himself if you turn the other way and stop looking at him.

3. Play Bill: Comes with a martini glass and a piano to lean on. Pull his string and he warbles the score from *She Loves Me* before breaking into tears for no good reason.

4. Chelsea Jim: Pull his string and he doesn't say anything because he's too busy checking out his own pecs.

5. Tommy the Top: You don't pull his string. He pulls yours.

6. Diesel Debbie: Comes with a crew cut and earrings that she never wears. Pull her string and she says, "Who needs a U-Haul? I'll be over in five minutes with my truck!"

As you can see from our last doll, we haven't forgotten our lesbian sisters, who also had a tendency to cross-play when they were kids. One friend of ours admits that her only interest in dolls was in building their homes. One year, she actually built a five-foot A-frame for her little plastic friends, and she often wondered why Barbie came with everything but a power tool set.

Another toy for gay boys of all ages might be the Gay Jock in the Box. There could be a picture of Greg Louganis on the side, and every time you turned the crank, a closet door would open and another star athlete would come popping out. An older game that could use some updating is Pin the Tail on the Donkey. First of all, how many kids have ever seen a donkey? What we need is a game called Paste the "Silence Equals Death" Sticker on the Outdoor ATM Machine. The goal of this game would be to get as many of these stickers as we can on phone booths, telephone poles, and traffic signs without being caught by the police.

In addition, we could use a whole new batch of coloring books and activity books for gay kids. For one thing, all those Venus Paradise Coloring Sets didn't quite cut it. We grew bored with them quickly because no queer kid really wanted to be told what color had to be used where. And, finally, why not paper dolls for budding drag queens? Every set would come with three cardboard drag queens, six wigs, and twelve stunning evening gowns, which are all too tight to zip up in the back.

Chapter 5

Fairy Tales

*M*any gay children coped with reality by avoiding it altogether and by escaping into fantasy. We all loved classic children's stories, such as tales from the Brothers Grimm and Mother Goose rhymes. Typically, however, we didn't always appreciate these fables from the conventional point of view. For the most part, because we felt ostracized ourselves, we rarely identified with the innocent, the naive, or the pure. Rather, we tended to feel more deeply for the downtrodden, the pushed aside, and the defeated. Thus the lessons we learned were rarely the lessons intended by the authors.

Take "Beauty and the Beast," for instance. If we look at it through the eyes of the heroine, it's an inspiring tale about the transformative power of love. From the point of view of the beast, though, the story seems to warn that you're not going to find your life partner until you lose some bulk, get rid of your facial hair, and go blond. While most people recall "Little Red Riding Hood" as a cautionary tale about a girl who meets a wolf when she wanders off the straight and narrow path, gay men will more likely understand this as the sad story of an unsuccessful drag queen who tried to impersonate a little old lady, but who couldn't pull off the illusion because his facial features were too big, fuzzy, and ugly.

We also often found ourselves identifying with the supposed villains of the story, preferring the evil sourpusses to the goody two-shoes. For instance, consider that poor little old lady who got shoved into an oven by those brats Hansel and Gretel. Sure, she may have been a little grumpy, but didn't she deserve a little credit for building a country home out of gingerbread?

And didn't we all feel just a little sorry for Snow White's evil stepmother? When your own mirror starts insulting you, it's time to get a new look. As for Snow White herself—a complete wimp. Her one redeeming quality was her ability to divvy up housework with a bunch of trolls she'd just met—a skill highly regarded by anyone who's ever had to share a house on Fire Island. Similarly, what gay kid didn't feel sorry for two of those Three Little Pigs who got gobbled up merely because they tried to build their houses out of something a little more exotic than cinderblocks. When did wicker become a crime?

How about Rapunzel? One bad hair day, and the engagement was off. And then there was the overly impulsive Sleeping Beauty, who married the first Prince Charming who kissed her after napping for a hundred years. Who could make a decision like that first thing in the morning? Wouldn't you think she'd have a cup of coffee before committing herself for life? Maybe she figured it had to be true love because this guy didn't seem to mind her morning breath after her not brushing her teeth for a century. After a hundred years of plaque, we're surprised that the Prince's head simply didn't burst into flames upon contact.

As for Cinderella, she married some guy from a one-night stand whose one redeeming quality was that he returned her shoe. In retrospect, though, this may be an admirable trait: In most gay trysts, if you leave an article of clothing behind you may as well kiss it good-bye, unless you spot it by accident.

One fairy tale, however, always made perfect sense to us: "The Ugly Duckling," written by the homosexual Hans Christian Andersen (who was played in the movies by Danny Kaye at the same time he was supposedly having an affair with Sir Laurence Olivier). The gay resonance of this tale is so obvious that it's hardly worth mentioning. An odd duck is hatched into a family of birds, which makes fun of him for being different. As time goes by this little misfit is revealed to have been a breed apart and evolves into a handsome swan who goes sailing off into the sunset with his equally gorgeous feathered friends. Nine out of ten gay men consider themselves heroes of exactly the same story.

In the main, however, as much as we loved this literature, its relevance was always in question. The problem was, it was written "once upon a time," when kings and queens still ruled kingdoms and most kids were growing up on farms. Mother Goose rhymes are another example of such a literary dinosaur. Most of them feature animals that the majority of kids have never seen, or else concern professions that no longer exist. When was the last time you met a candlestick maker outside of a lesbian crafts fair?

As gay kids we often felt doubly removed from these ancient ditties because, in addition to being feudal, they reflected a heterosexist social order. The poems may have been classic, but without any modern gay characters or themes we tired of them quickly. So—just for the fun of it—we authors have been tinkering with a few old nursery rhymes, bringing them up to date and refashioning them into a postmodern medley of actual gay life in America. Warning: The following poems are not actually for children, but they will be appreciated by the young at heart. We begin with a charming tale of life in the West Hollywood fast lane:

Three gay men,
Three gay men.
See how they run,
See how they run.
They all ran after the movie star
Who was cruising the guy at the end of the bar
Who wanted a foursome in back of his car
With three gay men.

Meanwhile, in Beverly Hills, Little Miss Muffet is ordering dinner in an outdoor café:

Little Miss Muffet
Sat on a tuffet
Eating her curds and whey.
"Why did I buy it?
I'm not on a diet.
Waiter, bring me the crème brûlée!"

While up in San Francisco, an old queen is having a hissy fit on a barstool. The bartender has had enough:

Mary, Mary, quite contrary,
Who do you think you are?
You've had your quota
Of Dewars and soda,
Now get your ass out of the bar!

While across the continent, in South Beach Florida, a young stud is surveying the scene:

Little Jack Horner
Stands on the corner
Cruising as guys go by
He sticks out his tush,
The guys go to mush
He thinks, "What a hot guy am I!"

While not far away in Key West, a middle-aged couple is trying to stay young and fit:

Jerome is in the counting house counting all his money.
Ramon is in the parlor eating bread and honey.
A trainer's coming to the house
To exercise Ramon
From all that bread and honey dear, his thighs have really
   grown.

While up north in Greenwich Village, a poor drag queen is making do in tiny living quarters:

There was an old drag queen who lived in a shoe.
Her home was a pump sized six hundred and two.
She thanked the good Lord that her feet were so big,
And stayed warm in winter inside of her wig.

Meanwhile, her friend down the block is going out for the evening:

Old Mother Hubbard
Always has rubbers.
She carries them under her shawl.
She knows safer sex
Doesn't always feel best
But it's better than no sex at all.

And in Northampton, Massachusetts, a lesbian is building an extension to her home:

Mary had a little lambda.
She wore it on her blouse.
And everywhere that Mary moved
She'd reconstruct the house.

While in Boston, a man and a woman—who never should have been married—are getting a divorce:

Jack and Jill
Were married 'til
The judge said they were through.
Jack had been
In love with Tim
And Jill was seeing Sue.

While that summer in Provincetown, a famous egg is trying to get in shape:

Humpty Dumpty tried to get slim.
Humpty Dumpty went to the gym.
He worked on his arms,
And he worked on his legs,
But still had cholesterol—being an egg.

Chapter 6

Horton Hears a Yoo-hoo

In the field of children's literature one man towers over the field like Shakespeare—the bard of children's books, the incomparable Dr. Seuss. The good doctor was a genius and, whether he knew it or not, his books were cherished by gay kids. Somehow, Dr. Seuss always managed to subvert the strictures of our dull everyday lives and to hold out the hope that, one day, we, too, would find a different world—a lusher world, a world full of surprises, a world that danced to a different drummer. In a brilliantly imaginative form, all the themes that would later inform our lives as gay men were right there in these books.

Look at *The Cat in the Hat.* He was like our first fabulous gay uncle: the one who shows up unexpectedly when our mother's not around. He is, in other words, the Auntie Mame of kids' books. The one who gleefully instructs us to break the rules, redecorate the house, and learn a new slang. He's the gay prototype for whom nonsense is everything, the eternally mischievous child with a slew of secret friends who help him out after he makes a mess of things. He's also hypersensitive to slights and has about as much tolerance for the real world as Blanche Dubois.

Then there was the hapless Horton—that one hundred percent faithful elephant—of *Horton Hears a Who* and *Horton Hatches an Egg*. Horton brought to mind the queer boy as the moral majority of one who stood up for what he believed. He alone was able to perceive an alternative universe that nobody else wanted to acknowledge. He was also the protector of the underdog, and though he was saddened by society's cruelty, he never gave up hope—he was the Mahatma Gandhi of kiddie literature. Another great queer figure was the title character of *The Grinch Who Stole Christmas*, who gazed upon conventional festivities with a hilarious mixture of envy and disgust. The grinch was every queer kid who ever felt angry or pushed aside at holiday time—who ever had that awful feeling that everybody had a place at the table except him. The world of Dr. Seuss was warm and inclusive, and bullies were always put in their places or gently reformed. In *Yertl the Turtle* Seuss mocked the straight male obsession with being at the top of the heap. In *The Lorax* he even took on environmental issues.

We also loved these books because they were so clever and because they rhymed. Before we discovered Cole Porter, Noel Coward, or Stephen Sondheim we had Dr. Seuss. And most of his characters looked absolutely fabulous! They had eccentric birdlike hairdos, impossibly long necks, bodies shaped like bottles, and clothes made of feathers. Each one was totally festive, and way over the top. Dr. Seuss also had the knack for taking the ordinary and using it to construct the fantastic. Look at *Green Eggs and Ham*—what could be gayer than a story about food presentation gone amuck?

Ultimately, Dr. Seuss was our first introduction to that grand artifice we would later call high camp. You can see his influence everywhere in our lives. Go to any Gay Pride parade and marvel at the bizarre costumes. Check out the pointy multicolored hairdos of the club kids. What about Lypsinka ... Lady Bunny ... RuPaul? Any of them could strut through the pages of Dr. Seuss's books and feel right at home. Where did we gay men first learn that every party should exceed the limits of our imagination? It was in Dr. Seuss's *Happy Birthday to You!*

Our favorite Dr. Seuss book, though, was probably that most complete ode to unbridled imagination, *To Think That I Saw It on Mulberry Street.* In that story, a little boy saw an ordinary street cleaner and embellished the incident into the most fantastic spectacle he'd ever seen. It was the ultimate act of taking the mundane and creating a fantasia—and it is in that spirit of joyful excess we present the following homage to our favorite author:

To Think that I Saw Him on Christopher Street

One day I was bored, I had nothing to do,
With nothing to do, you'd be bored. Wouldn't you?
So I sat by my window and feeling so sad,
Thought, "Maybe I'll answer a personal ad!"

But nothing delighted me, no little gems,
And why doesn't anyone like fats or fems?
So I left my apartment to find someone sweet,
And jumped on the subway to Christopher Street.

And once I got down there, I went to a bar,
I don't really drink—but that's where men are!
I saw guys who were hot, and guys who were not,
I saw guys drinking bourbon at four bucks a shot.

• • •

There were men wearing boots and men wearing sandals,
Men who were buff and men with love handles.
I saw guys wearing suede from their head to their toe,
And a couple of queens who had let themselves go!

Then one little jerk gave me such attitude,
That I told this young fellow, "I think that you're rude!
What makes you think that you're such a big deal?"
Then I snapped him three times and turned on my heel.

Out on the street, I looked to and fro,
I was looking for love but had nowhere to go.
But then from a distance I heard such a roar,
I'd never heard anything like it before!

Then down the street came the Gay Pride parade,
"With all of these guys I'm just bound to get laid!"
Then a huge cheer thundered up from the crowd,
Then the noises of engines. My god, they were loud!

It was everyone's favorite, the Dykes on the Bikes!!
Then came a new group—the Bikes on the Dykes!!!
These gals were bigger and these gals were bolder!
They carried their vehicles over their shoulders!

And on top of these bikes which were carried by dykes,
Were men who had recently come from the Spike.
They had rings through their noses and rings through their
    ears,
Rings through their toes-es and rings through their rears.

• • •

But my favorite had only one ring through his ear,
And up above that, through his head went a spear!!
And on top of this guy was a man with tattoos,
Of animals usually spotted in zoos.

He had a tat-two, a tat-three, a tat-four,
Had his shoulders been wider, he would have had more!
On his chest were his boyfriends from current to ex,
They called him the man with the Rolodex pecs!

His deltoids were pumped and his lats were so wide,
To get down the street he must turn to his side.
And next to this guy was a man with great abs,
Who works on the weekends all dressed up as Babs.

And up on their shoulders were singers in poses,
Who sang for us "Everything's Coming Up Roses."
They sang songs that were famous and songs that were
    rarer,
They kicked up their heels just like Chita Rivera!

And they carried these fellows all dressed up as nuns,
Who lifted their habits and showed us their buns!
And up on the nuns, at least twelve stories high,
Was a mountain of men rising into the sky.

First there were "chubbies," the guys who were fat,
Balancing "chasers," who like them like that.
There were gays from the Bronx, Staten Island, and
    Queens,
Gays from the Army and from the Marines.

●　●　●

I saw gays from Hawaii and gays from Formosa,
I saw gays from Australia and gays who lived closer.
And way up in the clouds was an army of Greeks,
Who are often drawn naked upon their antiques.

There were dozens of daddies, the bottoms and tops,
And hundreds of owners of novelty shops.
And the daddies wore leather! One guy was a wow,
I even saw one fellow wearing a cow!

And speaking of animals, who would have thunk,
I saw Horton who sported a ring through his trunk!
And Horton held hands with that nasty old Grinch
(Well you'd be mean too if you had only an inch!)

And on top of them all was the Cat in the Hat,
Smooching in public with Felix the Cat!!
Then all of a sudden the traffic was backed up,
'Cause down on the pavement sat marchers from ACT
    UP!!!

Then suddenly somebody called out my name,
His voice was more macho than Lucy's in *Mame*.
It was Bruno who played on the old football team,
I knew him in high school! This guy was my dream!

I told him, "Oh Bruno, I am quite in shock,
In high school, I always thought you a jock!"
And Bruno just smiled as he took off his shirt,
And he said, "Mary, please!" as he dished out the dirt.

"You ain't seen nothing. Just wait till you hear!
I'm not the only one from our school who is queer.

Remember Al Levy? Remember Bill James?
They're both on my team, cause we're in the Gay Games!

Remember Joe Johnson? He was such a geek!
Take a look at him now. He pumps five days a week!
And Marilyn Solkow, the Homecoming Queen,
Recently married a gal named Eileen."

Now it's hard to remember a word that he said,
Cause all I could think of was us two in bed.
And just when I thought I had no chance at all,
He asked for my number and told me he'd call.

A year later we're dating! We're really an item,
My friends are all jealous. I know how to sight 'em!
And I really love Bruno, so hunky and sweet,
And to think that I met him on Christopher Street!

The End

Starting Out:

Ages Five Through Twelve

"It's startling to discover at the age of nine in a world of Gary Coopers you are the Indian."

—James Baldwin

Chapter 7

A Day in
the Life

The next phase of our lives was our formal, difficult passage into patriarchal culture: That is, we began elementary school. Now, for some of us, this was a blessing. We enjoyed learning. We liked books. We loved papier-mâché. But for many others, leaving the relative safety of home to fend for ourselves amongst the rowdies of the world was an absolute nightmare, one in which we suffered frequent verbal and physical abuse. For a large percentage of sensitive gay boys, we not only wanted to be in the closet, we would have felt safer if they put a lock on the door.

But the truth is, we survived. Day by day we got smarter and learned how to cope as strangers in a straight land. We'd like all our readers to recall what it was like, that typical day in grammar school. It wasn't much different from any kid's school day, except that we were—maybe—just a little bit more sophisticated in our own naive sort of way.

6:45 A.M. Our mothers woke us up. Since many of us were dreamers, this sometimes took longer than usual. If only Mom had realized we were gay, she might have tempted us out of bed more quickly by yelling upstairs, "Wake up, honey. The Chippendale dancers are on *Good Morning America*."

6:53 A.M. We brushed our teeth. As kids who knew the value of a million-dollar smile, we were usually the first ones in the family to lobby for buying a Water Pik. We also tended to prefer the more flamboyant brands of toothpaste, the ones with sparkles or stripes. Being somewhat vain, however, we always brushed our teeth with the stripes going vertically, because we all knew the potential fashion disaster that could be wrought by horizontal stripes.

7:01 A.M. We got dressed. This was one of the most important decisions we would make all day. We wanted to look good but we didn't want to look too good, because that would get us beat up in the schoolyard. We gay boys usually wore the same basic clothes as our peers, but we figured out ways to make subtle fashion statements by buttoning the top button, or by tucking in sweaters that the other boys left untucked. Choosing our clothes was also one of our first opportunities to stand up for our rights. We knew what colors looked best on us. If we felt we were an "autumn," it would be that rust-colored vest or none at all.

We also knew the difference between good and bad leather. One friend reports that his parents sent him to an orthopedist because they worried that he was walking so stiffly. It turned out he was trying not to scuff his new Italian shoes. And speaking of buying new shoes, nothing beat taking that little runway walk and having the sales clerk squeeze our toes. This experience left an indelible impression on gay men all over the world. It was our first time onstage, and many of us later included the Buster Brown Shoestore on our acting resumes.

7:16 A.M. We ate breakfast. In those days, before we knew about Belgian waffles, we usually ate what the other kids ate—dry cereal. We also perused the backs of cereal boxes and were generally unimpressed. Items were offered for sale, but there was never anything that we particularly wanted to buy. Who needed a cheap ray gun? It would be several years yet before we got our first International Male catalogue and started purchasing anything through the mail.

7:32 A.M. We walked to school. On our way there we thought about the day ahead. We had a blotter and a letter opener for our desks. Our pencil sharpeners were always coordinated with our pencil cases. We were especially proud of our notebooks with pictures of movie stars on the cover. We were sometimes sad, though, because our mothers hadn't bought us everything we wanted. Somehow we hadn't been able to convince her that a thirty-five-dollar bottle of Vetiver cologne counted as a school supply.

7:45 A.M. We arrived at school early. We browsed some of the educational magazines spread out on the windowsill. Our favorite was *Highlights for Children* because of Goofus and Gallant. These two boys were total opposites. Gallant did everything right: He was considerate, responsible, neat, and respectful of adults. He reminded us of ourselves. Goofus did everything wrong. He was selfish, irresponsible, sloppy, and rude. He was the bad boy who gave us a little thrill.

8:10 A.M. We gave the teacher a gift. Seeing that the other kids were bringing the teacher apples, we went one step further. We brought her Baked Pears Alicia.

9:05 A.M. We participated in art class. Of course, we loved every chance we had to make our mother yet another useless gift. On this day we made a jewelry case by gluing macaroni shells to a shoebox and sprinkling glitter on top. Although we did our best, we were also very aware of the limitations of these materials. No matter what the teacher told us, we knew the difference between Ronzoni and Gucci. But we also knew that our mothers would have loved anything we made for them. We were like Picassos in their eyes, and all of our artwork was prominently displayed around the house. At great expense, our mothers had even saved all of our Etch-A-Sketch drawings.

10:02 A.M. We had a session with the speech therapist. The teacher had recommended us to this woman because some of us had slight lisps. In her dank little office she told us to count up to ten—and then she had us repeat "six" and "seven" over and over until we got them right. The truth was that we talked just fine—but that the speech therapist wore too much eye makeup, and her hairdo was ten years out of date.

10:41 A.M. We participated in show and tell. Today we brought in our *Playbills* from having seen Mary Martin in *I Do! I Do!* at the Broadhurst Theatre on 47th Street. The rest of the class had no idea what we were talking about.

12:16 A.M. We ate lunch. We carefully guarded our *Partridge Family* Lunch Box with Susan Dey on the side. We knew this would one day be a valuable collector's item—as very few would survive after their owners were beat up.

1:07 P.M. We played on the playground after lunch. As usual, the bad boys tried to build Molotov cocktails and blow up the school while we played "A My Name Is Alice" with our best friend, Margaret. We carefully substituted the word "girlfriend" for whenever Margaret said "boyfriend," but we knew we were lying. Later on some stupid student teacher organized a game of freeze tag so that the other boys could let off steam. We were tossed in with the ruffians. We were then divided into two teams, which the student teacher called the "Shirts" and the "Skins." We didn't know what he was talking about so we volunteered to be one of the Skins, thinking that we might get a lovely leopard print. Instead we had to run around with our chests exposed. We were mortified.

2:18 P.M. We went to the library. We loved it there. This was our sanctuary, because even the loudest boys had to be quiet as the librarian was tough as nails and as wide as the card catalogue.

2:47 P.M. We finally arrived back home. School was okay, but it really couldn't beat the freedom of hanging around the house with Mom. We checked *TV Guide,* hoping for a Hercules movie, but turned on the *Mike Douglas Show* instead, where some old actress was talking about having been born with a double uterus. We asked, "Mom, what's a double uterus?" She yelled at us to turn off the TV set.

5:06 P.M. We had dinner with our families. We liked the London broil and the Tater Tots, but we saw no reason for the mixed vegetables with lima beans. We refused to eat them and sat at the table snapping for the maître d' to come remove our plates. Our mothers were not amused. Once again, if only they'd known that we were gay, life would have been so much easier. Instead of threatening us they could have cajoled us by saying, "Honey, eat your lima beans. Liza eats her vegetables!"

8:36 P.M. We watched *That Girl* on television. This was our favorite show, because we were fascinated by the way she lived.

That night we dreamed that we'd moved to New York City and that our bedroom was really a studio apartment just like Ann Marie's—and that our parents were just the nosy neighbors who lived down the hall.

Looking back now we realize how unfair it was to deny gay kids access to gay-positive imagery. In all the years that Wheaties put athletes on their boxes, why wasn't Martina Navratilova ever represented? She's probably won more championships in her career than anyone, and she would have been a great role model for all kids—gay and straight. And where was Greg Louganis, the most popular figure at the 1988 Olympics, who, by bashing his adorable head on the diving board, sent thousands of gay kids scurrying for their sewing kits. We personally would have mended that wound shut! In order to compensate for this rampant homophobia—which has excluded anyone more questionable than Bruce Jenner from being featured on cereal boxes—we've put our heads together and come up with a few suggestions for adult breakfast cereals that could easily be marketed to the gay community:

1. Queerios—the first cereal to offer you the option of winning prizes by sending in either box tops or box bottoms.

2. Quentin Crisps—the frosted cereal for kids with frosted hair.

3. Cocoa Chanels—the cereal that gives you enough energy to be a supermodel.

4. Freedom Rings—the cereal that comes in all the colors of the Rainbow Coalition.

5. Totaled—the cereal for when you partied too much the night before.

6. Hell Raisin Bran—the cereal for those of you who like your roughage really rough.

7. Mister Crunch—the cereal for guys who work on their abs. If you send in ten box tops you can get a Mister Crunch slant board.

8. Special Kaye Ballard—the cereal that tastes great with second bananas.

and, finally,

9. Tricks—the cereal for boys who grew up just a little too fast.

Chapter 8

The Trouble with Angels
or, Gay Kids and Religion

I n general, most gay kids are profoundly affected by their early religious training. We're both more attracted by its positive aspects, and more repelled by its negative ones. The typical gay man thus goes through a fairly predictable cycle of first feeling deeply religious, followed by bitterly breaking away from conventional beliefs, and then finally settling into a lifetime of touring in *Godspell*. But all that aside—

In the beginning—

Many of us remember a honeymoon period during which old-time religion seemed to offer the possibility that life could be eternally magical and sacred. With its lovely fables conveyed in simple songs and colorful picture books, religion was a blessed escape from humdrum heterosexism. Of course, there were many rules and concepts we didn't understand, but we had faith that it would all make sense when we got older. Our first impressions of the deities were usually benign. Jehovah was a kindly granddad who sat on a cloud wearing a striped bathrobe, while Jesus was a sweet-looking kid whose head glowed in the dark. Organized religion also offered us socially sanctioned opportunities to own jewelry, such as rosary beads, and to play with dolls, such as miniature statues of the Virgin Mary.

Religion also gave us gay kids a chance to perform in choruses and recitations. These gigs eventually culminated in that one great chance at the big time—our confirmations and Bar Mitzvahs, at which we got to be divas. On such occasions we got all dolled up in iridescent sharkskin suits, took to the spotlight, and held the notes just a little longer than our straight counterparts. As far as we were concerned, these extravaganzas should have been listed in *Backstage,* and Clive Barnes should have been sitting in the first pew. We also had a lot more fun rechristening ourselves. In fact, one friend tells us that after being told that he'd have to choose a confirmation name after the name of a "saint," he almost chose "Eva Marie."

Religion also appealed to us because it made us horny. Ironically, all those injunctions against lust usually backfired. Most of us hadn't even been thinking about sex until some nun or rabbi informed us that we shouldn't be doing so. The Bible itself was pretty racy, because Bible folk lived in warmer climates and were usually pictured wearing fewer articles of clothing. For those of us raised Catholic, there were also sexy prayer cards with pictures of half-naked martyrs like St. Sebastian, who managed to look dreamy even while bleeding to death. In short, it wasn't surprising to us to learn that the phrase "knowing someone in the Biblical sense" refers to *shtupping* and not some common interest in scripture.

But then—

Eventually our attitudes began to sour. First we realized that most adults were even more baffled by religion than we were, and that the mysteries would never be adequately explained. At about the same time we began noticing that our parents were breaking the very rules we were being ordered to follow. Our mothers were hastily covering their heads with dish towels when it was time to light the Hanukah candles. Our fathers were cutting out of church early to avoid traffic. For them, church and synagogue were nothing more than cocktail parties from which one should never be the last to leave, while religion, itself, was comparable to fluoridation in the water—something supposedly good for us, although nobody knew why.

We lost our earlier sense of mystical wonder. Weekly services became an awful trial, and all that tiresome genuflecting felt like nothing more than The Pope's Physical Fitness Test. Bored by the sermons, we perused the church bulletins for ridiculous advertisements such as "McGregor's Funeral Parlor—Jesus rose again. You might not be so lucky!" And we began noticing that many of the adults directly in charge of our souls were pretty sorry specimens themselves. Typically, there were lushes like Father Jack Daniels, who all but kept a blender for mixing drinks in the tabernacle. During confession he'd be trying to cover up his booze breath with mints, which would have required a Life Saver the size of a Michelin tire.

Meanwhile, after-school religious instruction was becoming even more unbearable for us gay kids. In the late afternoon, when our blood sugar was lowest, we'd be forced to confront complex theological problems that had been confounding philosophers for millennia. This wasn't made any easier by the antiquated language being used by our teachers. We were never sure what "smite" meant. It sounded like a sissy verb to us, like God was pinching his enemies. And even more confusing was "brimstone," which sounded like some kind of tacky imitation brick. Was God punishing sinners with ugly outdoor siding for their homes?

More and more, God started sounding like some cranky older relative, the uncle who would smack us on our heads just for looking at his newspaper. His injunctions sounded increasingly capricious. If we were Jewish, God was so terrifying that we couldn't even write His name; we were told to spell it "G-d" so God wouldn't know we were talking about him—as though the King of the Universe were that stupid. Even the dumbest schmuck on "Wheel of Fortune" would have bought a vowel and figured it out. On the other hand, we Catholic kids resented Lent, when we were asked to sacrifice something yummy in commemoration of Jesus's forty days in the desert. Just because He had a lousy vacation was no reason we had to suffer!

But the biggest problem with organized religions was that they all had long histories of rejecting homosexuality. The sad truth is that our three major faiths—Protestantism, Catholicism, and Judaism—all seemed to agree on one thing and one thing only: As much as they disliked each other, they disliked gays even more, and it wasn't long before we queer kids simply gave up and tuned out. We were galled at the hypocrisy of church teaching and, if one more priest or rabbi tried to inform us that it was okay to be homosexual as long as one didn't practice homosexuality, we wanted to reply that it was okay to be religious as long as one didn't practice religion.

Catholics: What most gay men remember about being raised Catholic was going to confession, which was a nightmare of wasting time, fibbing, and feeling more guilty than we did before we went in. First, we had to choose which door to enter because we wanted the handsome young seminarian rather than the mean old codger. This was like "Mystery Date" for Catholics. Once inside the booth we waited for the little wooden panel to be slid aside and half expected Joanne Worley's head to pop through the wall. Then, wanting to keep our confessors on the edges of their seats, we struggled to come up with a few transgressions that would entertain our hosts without revealing our true sexual natures. Finally, we recited "Father forgive me, because I have sinned" and then launched into a litany of lies about coveting our brothers' toy soldiers and having impure thoughts about Debbie next door.

As Catholics we were also exposed to increasingly bizarre stories about statues of the Virgin Mary that bled and cried and did everything but order out for veal parmigiana heroes. We Catholic gay kids also had to deal with a pretty frightening picture of the afterlife, for in this most organized of all the organized religions, there was a place in Hell for everyone, and everyone had his place. Hell was described to us, at various times, as holding one's hand over a flame, licking a waffle iron, or spending our summer vacations in a microwave. This morbid view might have been dismissed as fantasy had the Church not then backed up its promise of eternal torment by subjecting us to twelve years of education by sadistic nuns.

Now, Catholic school gave many of us nightmares, and we were eternally haunted by the Lives of the Saints. If we forgot our homework we would imagine ourselves being torn apart by lions. In health class we half expected to be taught first aid for stigmata. And science projects were the worst, because we'd lie awake nights fearing that our model of the solar system would get us excommunicated. But most disturbing of all was the miracle of the Virgin Birth. Many of us didn't comprehend this event, because we didn't understand the natural mode of conception, much less the supernatural. But secretly we suspected that God's impregnating Mary was no more miraculous than the idea that we would ever do the same to a woman.

Meanwhile most of us had the sneaking suspicion that many of the priests were as gay as we were—which later turned out to be absolutely true. If *Going My Way* had been a more realistic depiction of parish life, Father O'Malley would have been played by Truman Capote, and the script would have been about a priest picking up a hitchhiker. Because of this, the Catholic Church, in spite of everything, often looked like a good place to work, and many of us envisioned the priesthood as a viable career option. The number of gay men who actually studied to become clergymen is astounding and, to this day, one can't throw a string of pearls on Fire Island without hitting a former seminarian. If nothing else, any religion that burned as many candles as Catholicism was bound to appeal to our romantic side.

Not only was the Catholic Church homophobic, but it was also sexist. Women were not allowed to become priests, a fact that confused many gay children who often came from families where our mothers had much more spiritual authority than our fathers. Later on we had to listen to the Pope explain that women were denied priesthood because none of the Apostles was a woman. Had he ever considered the fact that none of the Apostles was Polish, either? We authors believe that the real reason the church doesn't allow women to become priests is that they would then have to allow men to become nuns, and the convents would have to make way for Sister Herbert and Sister Brad.

Protestants: Most of us mainstream Protestant gay kids had it a little bit easier than Catholics. We didn't have the Pope to deal with, but we still had Sunday school, where we studied the Bible with all its inconsistencies. Most of us remember finding our first blooper in Genesis. Adam and Eve had only two sons, and yet they managed to populate the Earth. Hmm. Whom did Cain and Abel marry? Their mother? If this were an actual family, we surely would have read about them in the *National Enquirer*. Then on the next page, Cain killed Abel because God preferred Abel's lamb dish sacrifice over Cain's garden salad.

For many gay kids, this story was particularly resonant, because who but a testy queen would lose control over a recipe?

Some gay Protestants, on the other hand, had the gross misfortune of being raised by Fundamentalists. Fundamentalist preachers read the Bible selectively, claiming its authority for hatred and intolerance, while ignoring any injunctions that might put a cramp on their own lifestyles. Even as kids we saw through their hypocrisies. The truth is that the only time Jesus ever got angry to the point of physical violence was when he threw the money changers out of the temple. Many of us figured out quickly that we had more chance of getting into heaven than those greedy blowhards soliciting checks through the mail.

Many gay kids rebelled against Protestantism for purely aesthetic reasons. Church was simply boring, and Sunday school music was awfully unsophisticated compared to the Broadway cast albums we were collecting at home. Worse still, in the sixties many denominations tried to reach out to us kids by using corny folk songs, which we found even more repellent. To this day there are millions of Protestant gay men who still dream about being forced to wail "If I Had a Hammer" in front of their local Methodist Youth Groups. There were also those quasi-Christian love songs, like Debbie Boone's "You Light Up My Life," which drove more of us into secularism than Billy Graham and Jimmy Swaggart combined. To alienate us even further, at the same time that religion began borrowing from show business, show business began borrowing from religion. In the early seventies a plague of Broadway musicals raided the Bible for librettos; *Jesus Christ Superstar,* for instance, tried to reinvent the Son of God as an iron-lunged singer who belted his gospel—a kind of "Merman on the Mount."

Jews: Meanwhile, we Jewish kids were having our own problems. First of all we had those awful stories of Abraham, a charmless intransigent who smashed his neighbors' idols and was willing to shish-kebab his kid in order to satisfy some voice coming out of the sky. Even more frightening was the tale of Lot, whose wife was turned into a pillar of salt. For many gay boys this story engendered an awful terror that we'd wind up as a seasoning, not to mention the fact that with such a high sodium level, this woman's blood pressure probably went through the roof.

Judaism, however, did have several advantages for gay kids. For one thing, there were so many bizarre commandments that the straight kids wound up feeling just as confused and unhappy as we did. Also, gay sex wasn't considered such a horrible sin in the Jewish scheme of things. The real sin was eating nonkosher food. In other words, for Christians, your body is dirty, and you shouldn't have unclean thoughts about other men. For Jews, a pig's body was dirty, and you shouldn't have unclean thoughts about Canadian bacon.

Eating the right foods was of utmost importance, and there was one basic rule—we didn't eat anything that tasted good. Rather, we ate things that were supposed to remind us of a time in history when we were totally miserable. On Passover, for instance, we snacked on something called *charosets,* a thick, gooey paste that was intended to recall the mortar used to build the pyramids when we were slaves in Egypt. In short, we weren't happy until our jams tasted like cement. Another big Passover treat was matzoh, which was actually bread resembling balsa wood, because the story went that there was no time for the bread to rise when the Jews rushed out of Egypt. Well, we Jewish kids were a little suspicious because we had never seen our families rush out of *anywhere.*

Still, we had to put up with our own share of Jewish homophobia. If nothing else, we had to cope with that one scary sentence in Leviticus which stated that "thou shalt not lie down with a man the way one lies down with a woman," which is why so many of us thought we'd have to go through life making love standing up. Also, because Jews were in the minority, there was always the pressure to "go forth and multiply," which we were unlikely to do outside of math class. And finally there was the burden of getting married and carrying on the family name— which seemed impossible unless Tony Tortelli somehow managed to get pregnant and change his name to Schwartz. The net result of all this anxiety was that many orthodox gay Jews chose to remain in the closet their entire lives, often desperately clutching two sets of dishes.

In the final analysis, what made any of the organized religions' disapproval of gays so completely galling was that we gays have made so many artistic contributions to churches and synagogues. Anyone who doubts this fact should rent *The Agony and the Ecstasy,* in which the supposedly heterosexual Michaelangelo was hired to brighten up the Sistine Chapel. And for those of you who doubt that Michaelangelo was gay, consider the following: First, he loved big muscles—even his Virgin Mary looks like she's been working out at Gold's Gym. Second, Michaelangelo spent four years painstakingly painting one room. If he'd been straight, he would have thrown up some mahogany paneling and called it a day.

In the meantime we can only pray that Judaism, Protestantism, and Catholicism pick up the pace, get with the program, and open their doors wide enough to include everyone. Gays should simply be accepted for the roles we've always played in the spiritual life of mankind. Instead of being shamed, we should be shamans—we should have our rights *and* our rites. And some day gay kids will be taught that our souls are every bit as holy as the next guy's. Until this happens we can just strive to have more faith in ourselves and defend ourselves against quasi-religious folk who merely want to scare us. The next time some Bible thumper stops us on the street and demands, "Are you ready for Judgment Day?" we should just look him in the eye and say, "No, I have so much shopping to do!"

One of the more bizarre rules we encountered as children was the injunction in Leviticus against wearing fabrics woven from two different types of material. What a useless rule! First of all, what would the punishment be for disobeying? Would God thunder at us, "Thy laundry shall be accursed, and thy colors shall bleed unto thy whites"? Also, as gay kids we had nothing to worry about because we generally preferred 100% cotton and virgin wool. The truth is that if the Jews are the "chosen people," then gay men are the "choosy people," and it would be far more likely for a fundamentalist to burn in hell for his polyester than for us to be caught dead in a tacky blend.

In our opinion, the whole idea that God would be particularly interested in our clothing is totally absurd. There are, after all, more important things for God to do, like keeping his eye on the planets or watching out for Newt Gingrich. And yet there are several religious sects that believe that the Almighty is more obsessed with fashion than Diana Vreeland. The Amish, for instance, believe that they must maintain the historical fashion moment of when their religion was founded. Then there are the Hasidic Jews, who still dress like their first rabbi, who lived in eighteenth-century Poland. All we can say is thank goodness this rabbi didn't live in 1970's America, or we'd have a lot of elderly Jewish men running around Williamsburg in leisure suits and platform heels. Then every Friday at sundown the women would be lighting candles and singing "Shabbos Night Fever."

In short, the whole link between spirituality and clothing seems hard to justify. But if it could be, we could probably do the Old Testament one better and come up with a few suggestions for His Fashion Commandments:

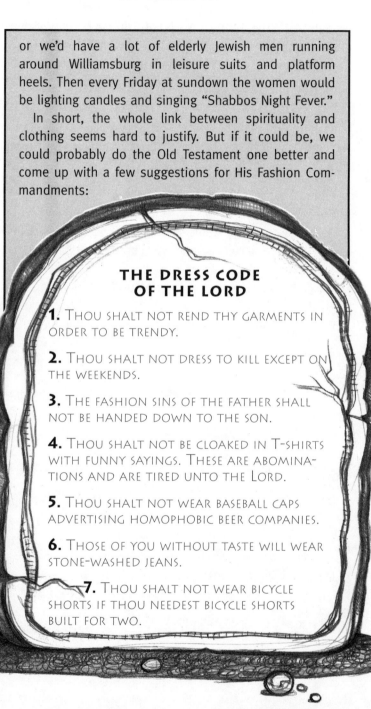

THE DRESS CODE OF THE LORD

1. THOU SHALT NOT REND THY GARMENTS IN ORDER TO BE TRENDY.

2. THOU SHALT NOT DRESS TO KILL EXCEPT ON THE WEEKENDS.

3. THE FASHION SINS OF THE FATHER SHALL NOT BE HANDED DOWN TO THE SON.

4. THOU SHALT NOT BE CLOAKED IN T-SHIRTS WITH FUNNY SAYINGS. THESE ARE ABOMINATIONS AND ARE TIRED UNTO THE LORD.

5. THOU SHALT NOT WEAR BASEBALL CAPS ADVERTISING HOMOPHOBIC BEER COMPANIES.

6. THOSE OF YOU WITHOUT TASTE WILL WEAR STONE-WASHED JEANS.

7. THOU SHALT NOT WEAR BICYCLE SHORTS IF THOU NEEDEST BICYCLE SHORTS BUILT FOR TWO.

Chapter 9

Putting the Bible
Through DeMille

Every gay child actually has two forms of religious upbringing. First he's raised in the faith of his parents. In addition, he then sees all the movies he can with biblical themes. Sooner or later these two educations tend to blur in our minds. It's as though the Shroud of Turin were created when Jeffrey Hunter blotted his makeup while making *The King of Kings*.

Hollywood has a long history of teaching us the path of righteousness. In the forties we had movies like *Going My Way* and *The Bells of St. Mary's*, which featured kindly priests and sweet-tempered nuns. Unfortunately, these movies were made by producers like Louis B. Mayer who were Old-World Jews and knew absolutely nothing about Catholic parish life. Then in the fifties Hollywood started making lurid costume epics like *Quo Vadis* and *The Robe*, which were basically opportunities for Hollywood actors to show off their muscles and for big-breasted Italian women to wear see-through chiffon. By the seventies, Hollywood started portraying the

Catholic Church as a metaphysical exterminator useful in getting rid of pesky demons and other assorted wickedness. Holy water was generally thrown around in these films as liberally as seltzer in Three Stooges comedies. Perhaps the perfect example of this genre is *The Exorcist,* in which so much water was splashed on Linda Blair that the part should have been played by Flipper.

Of course, the greatest biblical filmmaker of all was Cecil B. DeMille and, for gay men growing up in the fifties, he was more influential in teaching scripture than Billy Graham and Cardinal Spellman combined. Ironically, this man who thought he was documenting the Bible was in fact documenting the sexist attitudes of mid-century America. His stodgy, straight white males seem about as trustworthy today as the Nixon administration, and his biblical women were either exaggerated vixens or bland helpmates who would have made June Cleaver look daring. DeMille's epics from the fifties were also fairly accurate recordings of bad acting circa 1920, because the director, who began his career in movies shortly after Edison invented the medium, invariably made his actors grimace and react as though they were still in silent films. Even his best actresses, like Dame Judith Anderson, came across looking like Theda Bara on a bad day.

In this context, mediocre actors like Victor Mature and Hedy Lamarr, who played Samson and Delilah, looked totally helpless, not to mention miscast. Mr. DeMille, who was nearly seventy at the time, may not have noticed that Ms. Lamarr was a little long in the tooth to play the legendary temptress. Mr. Mature, on the other hand, was more of a chunk than a hunk. Lumbering along in his girdle, this Samson looks as if he would have brought mint jelly to the roasted lamb sacrifice, and, in his rush to the dinner table, might have knocked down the Philistine temple with his flabby thighs. But at least this story had a gay theme: "One bad haircut and your whole world can collapse around you." Of course, this plot was not completely true to life: In reality, as soon as a gay man begins to lose his hair he starts going to the gym, and he actually gets bigger and stronger.

But for us gay boys, the one DeMille movie that stands out among the rest is that truly elephantine epic *The Ten Commandments*. First, it had an all-star cast, all of whom had seen better days. Yul Brynner, still riding high from *The King and I,* strutted nobly and had a great chest, but he wore hats that even Carmen Miranda would have rejected for being too garish. The Pharaoh, played by wheezy old Sir Cedric Hardwicke, looked about as imposing as Jerry Van Dyke, and Yvonne De Carlo, who played Mrs. Moses, was only slightly less believable than she was years later as Lily Munster.

And then there was our least favorite actor, Charlton Heston, who played the great Jew himself, in casting that was about as plausible as Woody Allen's playing George Washington. For the life of us, we can't figure out how this terrible actor got his bony face into every biblical movie imaginable. Why, at the time it was even rumored that he and Audrey Hepburn were actually neck and neck for the lead in *The Nun's Story.*

Even against such competition the one truly great/awful performance in *The Ten Commandments* was given by Anne Baxter as Nefertiti—the fifties bad girl gone Egyptian. Her voice was so breathy in this role that even today our TV sets fog up whenever she's onscreen. She also had the regrettable habit of pouring her whole heart and soul into lines that would have been better off unheard. Our personal favorite was when she cornered the leader of the Jews in her boudoir and, with a great flourish of silent-screen acting, whispered seductively into his ear, "Oh, Moses. Moses. They call you a man of God. But I know you better than that!"

We also loved those ridiculous scenes in which God let his wrath fall upon the Egyptians, our favorite being when the Jews smeared lamb's blood on their portals to evade the Angel of Death. From this we learned the decorating principle of contrasting trim on doorways and windows. But by far the best part of this movie was its ending, when Moses goes up the mountain to receive the Ten Commandments, while the Israelites stay behind and party with Edward G. Robinson, performing what the narrator called "vile affections."

What makes this scene so hilarious was that back in 1957, the censors wouldn't allow "vile affections" to be shown in the movies, so twenty-five thousand extras were reduced to giving each other piggy-back rides and swinging their heads around like the June Taylor dancers. We can only guess how many of us kids believed that all this senseless writhing was actual sex. Think about it. When was the last time one of your dates tried to climb up on your back, feed you grapes, and groan ecstatically for no reason at all?

Chapter 10

Long Day's Journey into Silent Night

As we mentioned in the preceding chapter, gay men have always contributed to religious life: We wrote the hymns. We designed the cathedrals. We choreographed the Masses. And as children we invariably played the leads in our annual Nativity plays. Think of it this way: Wherever you have religion, you have ritual. Wherever you have ritual, you have theater. And wherever you have theater, you have some little Homo cabaretpien rehearsing his heart out and trying to put on the best darn show he knows how.

Ah, the theater! It has always been one of the few institutions in Western civilization that has provided a welcome home for our unique joie de vivre. Maybe the reason that we love the theater so much is that, having to pretend that we're straight, we learn character acting from birth. Or maybe we simply find life so dull that we welcome any opportunity to enhance, embellish, and overdramatize.

Drama club was, for many of us, an unofficial Headstart Program for Homosexuals, but rather than write an essay about our

love of the theater, we offer a little play instead. It's the classic
backstage melodrama of Francis Gumm—a tough little third
grader in a New York City Catholic school—and his yearly
attempt to produce the greatest Nativity play ever. Curtain up!
Light the lights! As a tribute to the unique sophistication and
savvy of the kiddie-show queen, we now present the following
musical extravaganza:

ACT 1. Scene 1.

7:30 A.M. The cafeteria of Our Lady Sings
Sondheim, the Catholic Elementary School for the
Performing Arts. FRANCIS GUMM, an eight-year-old
with moxie sits smoking a candy cigarette and
yelling at his mild-mannered assistant, LOWELL,
who's taking notes with crayons.

                    FRANCIS
We need a title for this year's Nativity
play. Read me what you have.
                    LOWELL
How about, "Our Fair Lady"?
                    FRANCIS
Close.
                    LOWELL
How's this? "I Never Sang for My Father Who
Art in Heaven."
                    FRANCIS
Too downbeat.
                    LOWELL
I got it! I got it! "The King of Kings and I."
                    FRANCIS
Perfect! I'm a genius! Now read me back the
casting notice.

Lowell adjusts his glasses and reads primly.

> LOWELL
> Wanted: Second to fourth graders who move
> well for the annual Nativity play. Cast break-
> down: Mary, Mother of Jesus. Must have that
> one-in-a-million smile to be pleasing to Jeho-
> vah, the creator of the universe. Jehovah,
> father of Jesus. Rugged offstage voice. Joseph,
> stepfather of Jesus. Must also know carpentry.
> May be asked to help build the set.

> FRANCIS
> The set! That reminds me. Where the hell is
> Vance?

VANCE VAN BUREN runs in. If he flamed any
higher he'd set off the sprinkler system. He
lays his plans on the table.

> VANCE
> Lowell, darling. Sorry I'm late. Anyway,
> voilà! I was up all night with my Magic Mark-
> ers. Here is your set! I see a lavish barn
> with stars atwinkle. We'll build the manger
> out of Legos, and here are my designs for
> Mary's costume changes.

> FRANCIS
> Hmm. Do you really think she needs a little
> black cocktail dress?

> VANCE
> Francis, darling, it's Christmas, and her
> son's birthday. She has to look fabulous. By
> the way, when are you casting?

                    FRANCIS
 I'm having auditions this afternoon in the
 auditorium.
                     VANCE
 Can't wait to see what hunks are playing the
 shepherds this year. And I'm sure you'll find
 the perfect little darling to play the baby
 Jesus.
                    FRANCIS
 I'm playing Him myself. I shall direct and
 star in my own production this year.
                     VANCE
 Well, excuse me, Miss Yentl. No offense, but
 you're no Babs.
                    FRANCIS
 No, but I am Francis Gumm, and my name still
 sells tickets in this school. Why they're
 still raving about my show and tell from last
 year, and I've got the review in *My Weekly
 Reader* to prove it. And don't you forget it!

 Scene 2
 That afternoon in the school auditorium.
 Francis is seated in the audience. Lowell is
 onstage at a table piled high with class photos, which were submitted in lieu of 8 x 10's.

                    FRANCIS
 Who's next?
                    LOWELL
 Chazz Johnson.
                    FRANCIS
 That little Theresa. Let him in.

CHAZZ JOHNSON flounces in. He's a six-year-old wearing an alligator shirt and a sweater tied around his shoulders.

                    CHAZZ
Oh, Mr. Gumm. I just have to say that it is such an honor to have the chance to audition for you. Your production last year of *Palm Springs Sunday* at Saint Catherine's was what theater's all about.
                   FRANCIS
Thank you. Now who would you like to read for?
                    CHAZZ
I'd like to play Joseph.
                   FRANCIS
Really? He's a pretty rugged guy.
                    CHAZZ
Is that a problem?
                   FRANCIS
Listen, kid, no offense, but you're a little light in the sandals for Joseph.
                    CHAZZ
Well, I could stretch.
                   FRANCIS
Gumby couldn't stretch that far. Joseph has to swing a hammer. The only thing I could see you swinging is a handbag.
                    CHAZZ
What should I do then?
                   FRANCIS
Don't quit your day job. Work overtime!
                    CHAZZ
I could play one of the shepherds.

FRANCIS

Which one—Cybil? Lowell let him play the innkeeper. He's more of a Paul Lynde type. Next!

CHAZZ exits. JANIE PLOOMERWITZ enters. She's a chubby little girl with a determined look. Lowell brings Vance the resume photo. Francis grunts disapprovingly.

FRANCIS

Is this a recent photo?

JANIE

It was taken last month.

FRANCIS

I see it didn't take you very long to pack on a few pounds. Pretty soon your eight by ten will be a sixteen by twenty. Listen, kid, these are baby pictures. If this photo had been taken any earlier, it would be a sonogram. Now who'd you like to audition for?

JANIE

I'd like to play Mary.

FRANCIS

Fat chance! You're not virginal enough. Next!

JANIE

But you never gave me a chance to sing!

FRANCIS

I heard you in choir. You stink! But tell you what, kid. The role of the cow is still open. Lose ten pounds, and it's yours!

JANIE breaks down sobbing and EXITS.

Next!!

FATHER SAM COHEN barges onstage. He's a
bald-headed priest smoking a cigar.

Who the hell are you?

                    PRIEST
Father Sam Cohen. I represent the little
girl you're about to see. Susie Flanagan.
                    FRANCIS
Can she act?
                   FATHER SAM
Can she act? Why she just finished the Patty
McCormack role in *The Bad Seed* at Saint
Helen's Drama Club.
                    FRANCIS
Hmmm. You think she can handle the role of
the mother of God?
                   FATHER SAM
Are you kidding? She could play Moses.
                    FRANCIS
Well, let's take a look at her.

SUSIE, a six-year-old peroxide blonde takes
the stage.
                    SUSIE
For my ballad I'd like to sing "Ave Maria"
and for my up-tempo I'd like to do "Hey Big
Spender." Hit it, boys!

The spotlight hits Susie. She belts out "The
minute you walked in the joint ... "

                    FRANCIS
 I think we have our Mary!

 Act II
 Two weeks later. Opening night of *The King of
 Kings and I.* Susie Flanagan's dressing room.
 SUSIE—dressed as the Virgin Mary in a little
 black cocktail dress—runs to her makeup table
 and throws off her wig in a huff. FRANCIS—
 dressed in Pampers for the role of Baby Jesus—
 runs in after her and tries to console her.

                     SUSIE
 I've never been so humiliated in all my
 life.
                    FRANCIS
 It was an accident. I swear.
                     SUSIE
 That cow stuck out her hoof on purpose! She
 was trying to upstage me. Did you hear her
 mooing during the Annunciation scene? She did
 everything but pull a quart of cottage cheese
 out of her udders! I'm leaving!
                    FRANCIS
 But half the parish is out there!
                     SUSIE
 Tell them to start praying.
                    FRANCIS
 The Mother Superior's in the front row!
                     SUSIE
 Well, Lazarus better be sitting next to her
 because you're gonna be raising this show from
 the dead!

SUSIE goes behind a screen to change her clothes.

                    FRANCIS
All right, all right. We'll make a few changes.

                    SUSIE
You can start with the script.

                    FRANCIS
It's from the Good Book.

                    SUSIE
I don't care where it's from. The book's no good!

A pair of high heels go flying over the screen and hit FRANCIS in the head. VANCE enters.

And another thing. You can tell Vance that his costumes stink. If this outfit were any cheesier I could use it for a tuna melt!

SUSIE emerges from behind the screen.

And look at you. You call those swaddling clothes. You walk out there in that diaper and half the audience will think you're June Allyson.

JANIE PLOOMERWITZ enters in her cow costume.

                    JANIE
I heard a commotion. Is there anything I can do to help?

SUSIE

Yeah, you can get lost, you Nativity scene stealer!

JANIE

You're just jealous.

SUSIE

You probably thought it was really funny when you started squirting milk at the wise men.

JANIE

Everything I did on that stage tonight was in character.

SUSIE

Including the cowpie at the end of scene two!

JANIE

It couldn't stink any worse than your performance. At least I prepared for my performance.

SUSIE

Is that why you spent the whole month grazing at the salad bar?

JANIE

I call it Method acting.

SUSIE

Well, I call it overeating. You'd put ranch dressing on a bale of hay!

JANIE

And if your performance was any more wooden you could have played the manger! Let's face it, you're washed up. You've been getting by on your looks, and you're not getting any younger!

FRANCIS
Ladies, ladies ...

FATHER SAM COHEN runs in.

FATHER SAM
Hate to break this up but, Susie, I got an audition for the next Barney video. We gotta leave now.

SUSIE straightens herself up and puts on a pair of sunglasses.

SUSIE
Hasta la vista, baby. I'll be on the Coast. If you want me, ring your cowbell.

SUSIE and FATHER SAM exit. FRANCIS and VANCE are dejected.

VANCE
This is a disaster!
FRANCIS
Who can we get to play Mary?
VANCE
How about Chazz?
FRANCIS
He's too effeminate.

LOWELL enters out of breath.

LOWELL
We have to start the second act! Mother

Superior is starting to heckle the ushers!

                    FRANCIS
It's no use. We'll have to close the show.

JANIE starts unzipping her cow costume.

                    JANIE
If that's the story, I'm bagging this
leather harness. It's steaming in here.

JANIE takes off her cowsuit and, to everyone's shock, she's much thinner.

                    LOWELL
Holy Jennie Craig!
                    VANCE
It's a fashion miracle. She lost twenty
pounds under that hide.
                    FRANCIS
Get into this cocktail dress. Janie, you're
our new Mary!
                    JANIE
But will they like me?
                    FRANCIS
Are you kidding? They'll be throwing their
Rosary beads on the stage. Baby, you'll be
going out there a third grader but you'll be
coming back a star—of Bethlehem!

JANIE exits to thunderous applause offstage.
VANCE pours ginger ale all around. CHAZZ
enters dressed as the innkeeper.

CHAZZ

Well, Mr. Gumm, you've done it again! They'll
be talking about this for the next two thousand
years!

VANCE

But first, gentlemen, a toast!

ALL

A toast!

FRANCIS

To life in the theater!

FINALE ALL SING

There's no business like show business
Like no business I know!
It's something that you really want to take up.
A little boy can really go to town.
With feather boas, glamour wigs, and makeup.
But please don't cake up
your sister's gown.
There's no people like show people,
They smile when they are low.
Yesterday you thought that you were all alone.
You worshiped Judy and talked like Joan.
Now you're in the theater
and at last you're home.
Let's go on with the show!!!

Curtain

Chapter 11

AC/DC Comic Books—Gay Boys and Our Superheroes

Most children learned to love reading from comic books, and we gay kids were no exception. Our favorites were those published by DC and Marvel that featured superheroes with secret identities. Of course, we gay children identified strongly with these characters because we were often leading double lives of our own. They were in the closet, and we were in the closet, however dimly aware of it we were at the time. Like young Superboy we had to keep our "special" skills to ourselves, and like the Incredible Hulk, we couldn't reveal our identity for fear that society would label us a monster.

Also, every superhero had his own personal villains, who fixated on ruining his life for no reason at all. And every superhero had obtained his powers in some fascinating way. Maybe he'd been born on Krypton, like Superbaby, or maybe he'd been been blasted by gamma rays or struck by lightning while working with strange chemicals. Maybe he'd been bitten by a radioactive spider. For those of us wondering why we were different, these comics offered a wide array of possible explanations.

And finally—let's face it—we loved these comic books because they were so inherently homoerotic and yet perfectly acceptable to read in front of our parents. Every superhero liked to wear tight-fitting Spandex, which showed off his pecs and abs—and yet we never even saw them drinking protein powder, bench pressing, or taking aerobics classes. All in all it might be useful to look at each superhero individually and discuss why we found them appealing.

Superman. He was *the* classic superhero, and his story was very relevant to the young gay reader. First of all, he came from another planet. Secondly, he was raised by some hick couple who were well-meaning but basically clueless. Then, like many gay men, he left his hometown of Smallville and traveled to a large city, where he got a low-paying job in a creative field. Then, while working at the newspaper, a co-worker got a crush on him, and he had to lie constantly about where he'd been and what exploits he'd encountered. Finally, there was some nerdy younger man tagging around after him, desperately trying to be his pal.

Unfortunately, there were many elements of this comic that struck us as highly implausible. First of all, we never believed that merely by putting on a pair of glasses, Superman would turn into a dork. His spectacles were actually quite stylish, and many gay men today would wear those frames even if their eyesight was twenty-twenty. Also, there must have been at least one gay man working at the *Daily Planet* who would have recognized Superman's body, no matter how boxy Clark Kent wore his suits (which is probably why we never met the paper's drama critic, who undoubtedly would have immediately spilled the beans to Lois: "Darling. Just look at Clark's shoulders …")

Spiderman. Spiderman was and remains fascinating because he was the most neurotic of all the superheroes and, in retrospect, the most gay. First of all, in Spiderman's everyday identity, Peter Parker, he was always presented as a hunky, troubled, insecure outsider who lay around his room shirtless, musing on his supposed inadequacies and worrying about his gray-haired aunt. Only gay men are that self-indulgently alienated and will take quite so much interest in their elderly female relatives.

Secondly, Spiderman's superpowers were about as queer as they could be. So what if he could climb walls? Frustrated gay teenagers have been climbing walls for years. Also, Spiderman ensnared villains by spraying webs out of his wrists, an ability about as butch as throwing doilies on a sofa. We know drag queens who could immobilize fag bashers with cans of Final Net hairspray.

The Incredible Hulk. The Incredible Hulk was the Dr. Jekyll and Mr. Hunk of the comic-book world. The premise was that Dr. Bruce Banner gets blasted by gamma rays, which cause him to bulk up in an instant as if he'd taken some kind of Frankensteroids. On the *Incredible Hulk* TV series, this transformation was accomplished by having Bill Bixby turn into Lou Ferrigno, a former Mr. Universe. This was all very sexy, as every episode would feature close-up slow-motion shots of Mr. Ferrigno's muscles bursting out of his shirt and leaving his pants in tatters. In fact, we believe this 1970s series may have inspired the ripped and torn fashions worn by gay men who, ten years later, were also transforming themselves into hulks.

Batman and Robin. Batman wasn't really a superhero. He couldn't even fly. Basically, all he could do was ride around town in a Batmobile and toss around a bunch of Bat gadgets that he made in his private toolshed. He was a straight boy's fantasy that, if you souped up your car and excelled in metal shop, people would be really impressed. The most interesting thing about Batman was his mysterious life as millionaire playboy Bruce Wayne. Think about it: This guy lived in a mansion with tons of antiques, hardly ever dated women, and kept a handsome young man for a ward. If as kids we didn't quite know what to make of this arrangement, as adults we have become familiar with it in places like Beverly Hills and Palm Springs.

The Fantastic Four. These four friends were all exposed to something in orbit that turned them into superheroes with different abilities, all which now seem uncannily queer. First, there was the Invisible Girl, whom any shy lesbian could identify with. The scaley Thing could have used a good moisturizer. The leader of the group, the Professor, looked as if he'd attended one too many stretch classes. And, finally, there was our favorite, Johnny Torch. When this guy wanted to go into action, he would yell to himself, "Flame on!" How many times as adults have we walked into a gay bar and voiced that very same refrain to ourselves?

Wonder Woman. Wonder Woman was for years the only female superhero around. This name fit perfectly because we always "wondered" what her *real* story was. After all, she was an Amazon who grew up on an all-women island off the coast of Greece ...

The Green Lantern. The less well-known Green Lantern was a major gay curiosity. Basically, he derived his powers from a ring he wore and a green lamp that he kept at home and cherished above all his other possessions. In short, he was the Liberace of superheroes, into major jewelry and home furnishings. We wouldn't have been surprised if this big Carol Ann turned up one day wearing a cape made out of ermine.

Flash. Flash, whose only power was the ability to look good in a red uniform and jog at supersonic speeds, was a good example of a guy who possessed one small talent that he tried to parlay into a major career in the big leagues. He was like the Vanna White of superheroes.

The Silver Surfer. This bizarre comic book was based on the premise of a superhero who flew on a surfboard. He had a special appeal to gay kids because he wore silver lamé and had a low-maintenance body that looked like Formica and could have been cleaned with Fantastik.

X-men. Currently, the most popular comic superheroes are Marvel's X-Men and X-Teens. The latter are a group of mutant teenage superheroes who are treated as freaks and outcasts by normal society, and so they've banded together to use their powers for good and to try to change society. Boy, doesn't that sound familiar? Our favorite of the X-Men is Wolverine, who has superstrong claws. Anyone whose nails are impervious to emery boards is pretty amazing in our book, although if you got him a temp job typing, he'd probably be all thumbs.

North Star. Recently an actual gay superhero made national headlines—North Star. This was certainly a breakthrough, and we look forward to scores of such characters in the future.

Archie. Superhero comics weren't the only genre to which we were exposed. There were also the "sit-comic books" about the supposed real lives of American teenagers. The most popular—

and most disappointing—of these was the Archie series, the only comics that made high school seem worse than it really was. We were asked to believe that two attractive, big-busted teenagers, Betty and Veronica, were in a bitter rivalry for the attentions of Archie, a red-haired geek with skinny legs. These characters were so badly drawn that they all seemed to have the same heads with different toupees, and to indicate that it was winter the artists did nothing but throw a few scarves and woolen hats on these teenagers who, for some reason, never seemed to wear coats. Who knows how many impressionable gay youths risked hypothermia just to make a fashion statement?

If Archie comics were decidedly nonqueer, Harvey's World Famous Comics featured characters who were all so queer they could have been written by Harvey Fierstein. If you're not familiar with this company, we only need remind you that these were the folks who gave us the likes of Little Dot, Wendy the Witch, and the following three characters, who all seemed like they would wind up gay adults:

1. Richie Rich. This lonely little boy was portrayed as being without a drop of malice, overprotected by his parents, cut off from the other children, and a natty dresser to boot. What would happen to him as he got older? Well, like most rich gay kids he probably would have had no interest in assuming his father's business, would sail around the world, and eventually wind up in South Beach, Florida. Here, he would fight and win a battle with the bottle, settle down with an exotic dancer named Luis, become best friends with Elizabeth Taylor, and donate most of his fortune to the battle against AIDS.

2. Little Lotta. This young gal was irrepressible, physically daunting, and unconcerned with what anybody thought of her.

After college she would finally come out of the closet, become a chiropractor, and start cracking bones for a living—including chicken and spare ribs. Eventually she would become domestic partners with Nancy, who had been unhappily married to Sluggo. Nancy and Lotta would then move to Montana, where they would promote Womyn's Music Festivals. Eventually, highly regarded for her organizational skills, Lotta would enter politics and become the first openly lesbian senator. In later years she would take up golf and be a big hit at the Dinah Shore Classic.

3. Casper the Friendly Ghost. This sad little victim of circumstances was admittedly odd, but we had to admire anyone with so high-pitched a voice who would still have the nerve to approach strange, burly men and whine, "Would you be my friend?" Luckily, he couldn't be fag bashed because fists would go right through him. Eventually, he would have to go where every eccentric queer inevitably winds up—New York City, where his bizarre appearance would make him a big hit every year at the White Party. Then, every Halloween he'd give his friends a hoot by dressing up as Mrs. Muir. Still unable to make real friends, he would try toughening up his image—but the tattoos wouldn't stick to him and the nipple rings would just fall right off his body. Finally, he would join the Chelsea Gym and buff up his physique, but he would continue to be frustrated, because no matter how big his shoulders got, his voice would still sound like it belonged to Beverly Sills. "Would you spot me?" he would ask in his breathy soprano, and his gym buddies would run away from him in horror.

QUEER READERS

Unfortunately there have been very few books written for gay children—or even books that would instruct children about how gay people live. Two of the best-known are *Heather Has Two Mommies* and *Daddy's Roommate*, which recently engendered controversy with right-wing Fundamentalists who, to paraphrase Lady Bracknell, didn't want to tamper with the natural ignorance of their children. Fundamentalists sought to ban these books because they feared that kids would be "recruited" into the so-called gay lifestyle. The fallacy of this argument is apparent: How many kids who read *Madeleine* were influenced to move to Paris and live with nuns?

In any event, as authors of gay literature ourselves, you can guess where we stand on this issue. We would welcome more gay books for children, starting with sequels to the two classics mentioned above. How about *Heather Has Two Mommies and They Both Coach Women's Soccer* or *Daddy, Do We Have to Watch* All About Eve *Again?* In the meantime, gay kids will have to satisfy themselves with show-biz biographies, the three most favored being *Weep No More My Lady* (Judy Garland), *Something's Got to Give* (Marilyn Monroe), and *Enter Talking* (Joan Rivers). And speaking of good horror stories, forget about Frankenstein and Dracula: We suggest you have a look at *Bette and Joan, The Divine Feud.*

Alternatively, gay authors could begin creating new works for gay kids. Why not take a few classic titles and alter them to make them more relevant? We might then see books like *Dr. Jekyll and Mrs. Heidelbaum,* about a young Jewish *fegele* who one day makes the horrifying discovery that he's turning into his mother. Or, how about *Voyage with a Bottom to the Sea,* about a young man's first trip to Fire Island? And how about those perennially popular series for young adults, The Hardy Boys and Nancy Drew? Has anybody ever thought of switching them around for gay kids? We could then have The Nancy Boys and The Hardy Girls. It wouldn't be too hard to imagine *The Nancy Boys and the Secret of the Hidden Magazines.* Or, *The Hardy Girls and the Strange Case of the Field Hockey Friendship.*

Chapter 12

The Games Gay
Children Play

Many gay kids loved board games because they
gave us a chance to compete without being verbally abused or physically endangered. Also,
board games required little exertion to participate
and, unlike most sports, were enjoyed in pleasant environments, such as shaded patios and cozy dens. We didn't need to
scamper breathlessly around bases or recklessly throw ourselves at an opponent. There was none of that awful desperation to make the team, and there was no horrible stigma if we
lost. We could never be the last one picked for Chutes and Lad-
ders, and if somebody beat us at Battleship, our fathers
wouldn't get depressed. Best of all, there wasn't that backlog of
humiliation and shame associated with athletics; if we sucked
at Monopoly two Christmases ago, nobody seemed to remember.

In short, board games were Competition Lite, and the best
thing about them is that they allowed us to triumph, for we were
just as likely to emerge victorious as the bullies and the jocks.
We didn't have to be outstandingly agile or physically gargan-

tuan to overcome our adversaries, but merely needed patience, luck, and some small ability to scheme. In fact, board games were previews to the real world, where the ability to accumulate property and cash is often far more important than the ability to catch a fly ball. From a politically correct perspective, however, most of these games were actually rather dreadful, as the majority of them required us to bankrupt our friends, suspect them of murder, or pursue world domination. In short, we were being trained to act like adults.

Monopoly: This capitalistic orgy is the most enduring of all the classic board games. Invented during the depression, it is a game of acquisition based on the idea "I'm okay. You lose!" The rules for Monopoly read like the platform for the Republican party, because the winner is the one with the most money and property, while all the less fortunate go bankrupt and homeless. On the other hand, Monopoly demonstrates that the reason free enterprise succeeded so well was that it was a lot more fun than communism. Try to imagine, if you will, a Soviet alternative to Monopoly called Collectivization, in which you got to become "The State" and organize communal farms. It would never sell.

Monopoly also had a complicated set of instructions printed on the inside of its box, and many gay kids remember inevitably being the nerd who read the rules, tended to the bank, and kept the other players in line. We were also a little more careful about choosing markers to reflect out personalities: Future drag queens picked the lady's shoe, musical comedy fans chose the top hat, and those of us bound for a career in the Navy chose the battleship cruiser. On the other hand, some of us had trouble playing the game because we weren't predisposed to rampant real estate consumerism. As gay kids, we were far more interested in quality than quantity, and our fantasy was to buy only one house and then spend all of our money fixing it up. But as the game wore on we eventually got into the spirit of securing entire neighborhoods, a skill we would later use in the name of gentrification. We were also adept at buying hotels, and many future bed and breakfast owners got their start increasing the value of Marvin Gardens.

In fact, we gay kids often learned to enjoy Monopoly so much that in the future, we'd like to see somebody invent a game called Queer Monopoly, that would prepare gay children for doing business in the gay community. In this game, Broadway would take up three-quarters of the board, and if we bought Reading Railroad, we could take tourists on a ride through the wine country. If we had the misfortune of going directly to Jail we could make the most of it by lifting weights and having a boyfriend named Noodles.

The Game of Life: This masochistic pastime was similar to Monopoly, but far more dismal. Another game of money and real estate, it also added the realistic possibility of personal misfortune, against which we were expected to buy increasingly expensive insurance policies. "Life," according to this game, was nothing more than an endless series of personal calamities, and every spin of the wheel could result in a fire, a car accident, or a disease. Whereas Monopoly encouraged us to be reckless entrepreneurs, The Game of Life was designed to show us what it would be like to grow old in a society without a national health program. Rather than being fun, it offered recreational anxiety, and made us so unhappy that many of us wanted to stop midway and prepare a living will.

For many gay kids, The Game of Life crystallized our intention to avoid following in the bourgeois footsteps of our parents. For all the trouble that "life" promised, the ultimate goal of living in a heavily mortgaged suburban mansion seemed terribly unglamourous against our actual dreams of traveling around the world, choreographing a ballet, and winning a Tony Award. Their Game of Life simply wasn't our game of life; and without any goals to excite us, this board game was truly a bored game.

Candyland: Unlike Monopoly and The Game of Life, this entry-level board game was for younger kids and could be finished in less time than it took to remove it from the box. Most gay men remember Candyland fondly because we played this game when it was still cool for us to hang out all day with our girl cousins. Unfortunately, Candyland was probably invented by dentists, because after staring all afternoon at pictures of Peppermint Forests, Ice Cream Floats, and Gumdrop Mountains, we were likely to go into sugar withdrawal and suddenly demand a field trip to Baskin-Robbins. In one bizarre instance the Heimlich Maneuver had to be applied to a chubby four-year old who had taken a bite out of the board. We can imagine nothing more sadistic, except maybe Cigaretteland, for addicted teenagers, which would be played on a gameboard resembling a carton of Viceroys.

Scrabble: The interesting thing about Scrabble is that it allowed young gay nerds and middle-aged women to sit around the community pool and compete as ruthlessly as junkyard dogs over a bone. In fact, this game, which required only two talents—a large vocabulary and a killer instinct—was perfect for young boys who would later want to be drama critics for the *New York Times.* Tempers generally flared during a Scrabble match, as one procrastinator with bad letters could hold up the game for days on end. In fact, one could have planted wheat in the time it took a slow player to maximize the use of four E's, a U, an X, and a J. Even more galling were those players who had never read a book in their lives yet handily won at Scrabble because they just so happened to be fluent in words that hadn't been used since the Phoenicians invented the alphabet—words like "proa" and "ut." Scrabble also provided the perfect opportunity to come out to our family and friends, as it not only afforded long silences perfect for personal revelations, but the "Q" in "Queer" was worth ten points, and so the temptation to spell it out was almost irresistible.

Clue: This English game of crime solving has the jury divided. Set in a genteel drawing room, Clue was perfect for hopeless gay Anglophiles who would later develop an addiction to Merchant Ivory movies. Clue was also interesting because it postulated that even the most conventional-looking blokes were capable of carrying deep, dark secrets. For us Sherlock Homos it was fun trying to guess the probable sexual orientation of the various suspects—such as the fey Colonel Mustard, who always appeared somewhat Dijon. On the other hand, Clue was rather grim for gay kids in that it gave the impression that the homicide rate in London was higher than that in the South Bronx. Many of us found the game tedious because life was mysterious enough without taking on the burden of doing police work. And finally, we question whether Clue has aged well, because we doubt that postmodern gay kids raised on the real life horrors of Court TV would get terribly excited over who bashed Professor Plum in the drawing room with a candlestick. In fact, Milton Bradley might even want to consider updating Clue, making Mr. Green a disgruntled postal worker with a high-powered rifle, Mrs. Peacock a crazy Mom plotting the murder of a cheerleader, and Mrs. White an abused wife pouring gasoline on the bed of her sleeping husband.

Risk: The delightful Risk gave us the charming illusion that we could devastate entire continents without leaving the comfort of our parents' den. Many gay kids played this game with great verve—which isn't too surprising, as Alexander the Great, the first man to have "World Domination" on his resume, was himself queer. The major drawback to Risk was that it gave some of us the hope that we'd one day be welcomed into the military. Another unfortunate side effect was that it encouraged megalomania at an age when we might not have known the difference between good clean fun and seizing the Sudetenland. On the plus side, we did learn global geography, which prepared us for planning exotic vacations. In fact, Risk afficionados remember that each country in the USSR was listed separately, so that long before the Soviet Union broke up, we had some familiarity with such obscure place names as Belarussia, Kamchatka, and Uzbekistan.

Mystery Date: The goal of Mystery Date was the chance to open a compartment in the middle of the board and find some cute guy on the inside—which meant that the real mystery was figuring out a way to play this girls' game so nobody knew we were gay. While the girls were hoping to find a "dream," we were just praying that nobody would label us a fag. In the final analysis, playing Mystery Date turned out to be very instructive for later on in life when, once again, our dates would come popping out of closets.

Nowadays board games must compete with high-tech video games. These new games are highly popular, in that they combine two boyish obsessions in one activity: They let youngsters watch TV, and they encourage them to blow things up. In fact, video games now make more money than the entire motion picture industry, so it's only a matter of time before business begins targeting the gay child.

Super Baby Jane Game: The action here is unrelenting as you become Blanche and battle your deranged sister, Jane. Navigate your wheelchair down the stairs as you try to get to the phone. Watch out! Jane's killed the housekeeper!

Teenage Mutant Ninja Ava Gardners: A group of gay teenagers is exposed to glamour and turns into a group of superpowered movie stars of the forties. The Ava Gardners are trying to get better parts in movies at Monster-Ghoul-Madmen studios, but Louis B. Monster won't let them go. Can the Avas do it? This game has nonstop back-stabbing action!

Super Drag Queens and Dungeons: This is the fantasy game that really lets you role-play. It has more swords and sorcery than twenty episodes of *Bewitched*. Fight the forces of evil that encourage homophobia.

Gymbo: He's gay. He's a soldier. He's got an AK-47. Try to kick him out of the military!

Chapter 13

The Gay World According to Ripley

Ripley's *Believe It or Not* was a series of books gay kids enjoyed just as much—if not more—than our straight friends. Mr. Ripley's matter-of-fact presentation of oddballs and misfits was oddly reassuring. The books also taught us facts about history, geography, anatomy, natural history, religion, and bizarre individual achievements. This series was always serious, funny, and silly all at the same time, and the sheer breadth of its inventory told us that the margins of normality were much more fluid than what we had thought. Most important, Ripley's never said, "These people were out of their minds" or "This guy's a lunatic." It was always respectful of the unconventional.

Just as we paid tribute to Dr. Seuss by updating his style to suit a modern gay sensibility, we'd like to provide the same service for Mr. Ripley. Below is a collection of bizarre, barely known facts that we authors have collected about gay life through the ages. We'd like to offer them for Ripley's next edition. Believe them or not!!

1. Todd Oskerman of West Hollywood, California, walked into a gay bar for the very first time, met the man of his dreams (a blond hunk with a great personality) who asked for his phone number and said he would call—AND HE DID! *Believe It or Not!*

2. Tina Thorndike of Northampton, Massachusetts, teaches gym, owns six cats, has seen K. D. Lang twelve times, coaches women's softball on the weekends, and is NOT A LESBIAN!! *Believe It or Not!*

3. Bruce Bibley of Cleveland, Ohio, started impersonating Carol Channing on February 3, 1923, ONLY THREE DAYS AFTER SHE WAS BORN! *Believe It or Not!*

4. Attitudes, a gay bar in Indianapolis, Indiana, has been playing the song "Gloria" by Laura Branigan nonstop since 1981, and NOT ONE PATRON HAS NOTICED!! *Believe It or Not!*

5. Lance Trevor of New Bedford, Massachusetts, has been sitting on the same bar stool, telling the same old tired stories, and NURSING THE SAME DRINK SINCE 1957. *Believe It or Not!!!*

6. Al Jackson, of Phoenix, Arizona, worked out for seven years and built a phenomenal body, but has never cut the sleeves off his shirt, never worn a tank top, and has NEVER GONE SHIRTLESS AT A GAY PRIDE PARADE! *Believe It Or Not!*

7. Todd Dotson of Brooklyn, New York, the stupidest gay man in the world, HAD TO HAVE HIS PARENTS TELL HIM THAT HE WAS GAY! *Believe It or Not!*

8. Raul Ortega of Fort Meyers, Florida, known to millions as "the gay alligator boy," was born on June 23, 1964, ALREADY WEARING AN IZOD SHIRT WITH THE COLLAR TURNED UP. *Believe It or Not!!*

9. Back in 1951, when homosexuality was still considered an illness, Vince Wexler of Rego Park, Queens, went to see Marlene Dietrich in Las Vegas and CHARGED HIS TICKETS TO BLUE CROSS AND BLUE SHIELD!!! *Believe It or Not!*

10. Otto Rheingold from Bavaria, a gay psychic with the power of telekinesis, could not only bend a spoon with his mind but HE COULD ALSO SET A FABULOUS TABLE FOR EIGHT! *Believe It or Not!*

11. Joshua and Jeremy Taylor, a pair of identical gay twins, were so simpatico that while Joshua was being spanked in Seattle, Jeremy would actually blurt out "HARDER, HARDER!!" in Boston. *Believe It or Not!*

12. Chuck Gernsey of Topeka, Kansas, was abducted by gayliens who examined his body and GAVE HIM A SOLOFLEX!!! *Believe It or Not!*

13. If a gay ant were the size of a human, he would be able to bench press over three thousand pounds. But in order to be popular with other gay ants, he would still have to WORK ON HIS CALVES. *Believe It or Not!*

14. The Great Gay Wall Unit of China—the largest buffet ever built—WAS A 3,000-MILE CHINA CABINET FILLED WITH MING PORCELAIN!! *Believe It or Not!*

15. Meanwhile, thousands of miles west, The Colossus of Rhoda, one of the seven gay wonders of the ancient world, was a three-hundred-foot statue of Valerie Harper in her best-known role, CREATED THREE THOUSAND YEARS BEFORE SHE WAS EVEN BORN!!! *Believe It or Not!*

AMUSEMENT PARKS

In the nineties amusement parks have begun instituting highly successful "Gay Days" during which adult gays and lesbians are encouraged to come and enjoy themselves. This is only fitting, because ever since childhood, we've been fascinated with these places. Whether it was a traveling carnival or a huge corporate theme park, these fantasy lands were tonics to suburban boredom, and we especially loved visiting them at dusk, when the neon signs flared with all the excitement of Times Square.

Amusement parks were often where we first experienced independence from our parents, whose aching feet and delicate stomachs prevented them from keeping up with us. It was also where we discovered that having fun meant getting maximally disoriented, scared, and queasy. In other words, trips to amusement parks were previews of our gay adulthood, when going to bars would once again require treading on sawdust, jostling our peers, and waiting six hours for that special four-minute thrill

that would make it all seem worthwhile. And for us budding leather queens, amusement parks were where we
first learned the excitement of being hoisted up and
strapped in. The worse we felt at the end of it all, the
better time we had!

But not everything was blissful at amusement parks
for the little gay thrill-seeker, especially younger boys.
The snacks, for instance, were generally nauseating and
had the nutritional value of styrofoam. Cotton candy
belonged to no discernible food group, and the hot dogs
were made from meat by-products so dangerous they
should have been labeled "bye-bye" products. Meanwhile, the best rides, like the roller coasters, were off
limits, even though the lines for these attractions were
so long that we could have grown three inches by the
time we got to the front. How we hated having to go on
the unsophisticated baby rides! The Tea Cups were a
complete bore, and even more humiliating was being
saddled on a half-blind pony with one hoof in the glue
factory.

The bottom of the barrel, however, was a completely
unconvincing House of Horrors. Typically, we would climb
into some rickety old carts and then ride for a few seconds in complete darkness. Then we'd hear some taped
ghost chuckles, and a few cheesy goblins would fly by.
Of course, as connoisseurs of the theater, we always
knew these creatures were nothing more than cheap Halloween costumes flouncing about on wire hangers. It
was like being locked in a darkened dry cleaners and
watching strange laundry being whipped around on
racks.

Nowadays, if they really wanted to horrify us gay

adults they could build a Queer House of Horrors, which would be nothing more than an actual replica of a standard suburban tract house. First, we would tentatively enter a vestibule carpeted in powder-blue shag. Then we would tiptoe warily down a plastic runner into the family room, which would have—gasp!!—an acoustic-tile dropped ceiling to better muffle our screams. Then we would be strapped into a velour recliner with plastic slipcovers, between two animatronic maiden aunts who would repeat the same sentence over and over again: "When are you going to get married? When are you going to get married? When are you going to get married?" *"Aaaaaah!!"* Nurses would have to be in attendance for those of us with weak hearts.

Chapter 14

Queeries

or, Snappy Answers to Obnoxious Questions

The worst thing about gay childhood was being forced to spend time with homophobes with whom we had nothing in common except a few chromosomes. Week after week, we were dragged to family gatherings and exposed to relatives whom, once we came out of the closet, we avoided completely. And because we were defenseless kids, they felt they had the right to butt into our business and regale us with their stupid opinions, which they foisted off on children only because no self-respecting adult would listen to them. Now, back then, we didn't have the political context to know we were being verbally abused. Nor did we have the wherewithal to flee from excruciatingly bad parties. We simply had to sit there and take it. Well, we authors do remember some of the ridiculous questions we were asked, and we've come up with some nifty answers we wish we had thought of back then. Now, stupid questions generally came in two major categories.

First there were those leering queries that assumed we were heterosexual. How we hated those situations in which adults

saw us playing with our "friends-who-were-girls" and assumed
that they were our "girlfriends." They would then brazenly project onto us all their own unfulfilled romantic dreams. What
adults didn't realize is that they were far more interested in our
supposed sex lives than we ourselves were. The truth is, homosexuals do not recruit; heterosexuals do. In fact, heterosexuals
were so adamant about recruiting us to their way of life that the
only way we could have escaped this draft was by applying for
status as a conscientious objector. So whenever some uncle or
older cousin asked us,

"Is she your first girlfriend?"
—we should have replied,
"Actually, I just realized I'm gay, so she's my last girlfriend."
—or,
"Are you two serious about each other?"
—we should have replied,
"No I'm just using her to get to her Barbie doll."
—or,
"When are you two going to get married?"
—we should have replied,
"Maybe when I get over my crush on Wesley Snipes."
—and, finally,
"Don't you want to have kids when you grow up?"
—we should have replied,
*"Only if I had a reliable boyfriend and a two-bedroom
apartment."*

Even worse were those questions that openly criticized our
masculinity under the mistaken notion that a young boy should
be weaned away from being graceful, imaginative, or nurturing.
Our society disapproves of so-called effeminacy so completely

that even complete strangers would stop what they were doing
in order to express their displeasure, and whenever they asked
us dumb questions like,

> *"Why are you playing with your sister's dolls?"*
> —we should have replied,
> *"Because my cheap parents won't buy me some of my own."*
> —or,
> *"Why do you throw like a girl?"*
> —we should have replied,
> *"I wish. Lesbians are great at softball!"*

Or, if some distant aunt tried to shoo us out of our own
kitchen by asking something like,

> *"Don't you think the boys shouldn't be in here with the
> ladies?"*
> —we should have replied,
> *"Shall we all go to the living room instead?"*
> —and, finally,
> *"Why don't you go play with the boys?"*
> —we should have replied,
> *"Well, if you insist ..."*

From Queer to Eternity:

Classic Gay Television and Film

"I can't remember a single thing I learned in ninth grade French or Science but I can still remember how much it cost to fly chili from Chasen's in Beverly Hills to the *Cleopatra* set in Rome."

—Paul Monette, *Becoming a Man*

Chapter 15

The Gay Kid's Guide to Television

or many gay men, our first homosexual experience was traumatic—we saw Truman Capote on *The Tonight Show*. Television is actually such a powerful medium that everybody, gay and straight, can point to a moment when their whole world was changed by what they saw on the TV screen. For the baby boomers, it was the death of JFK. For the generation Xers, it was the Challenger disaster. And for kids growing up in the nineties, it was the horror of seeing Faye Dunaway in a sitcom. Will we ever recover?

But, in general, nobody loved television more than gay kids, because, as dull as some shows were, they were still an improvement over our actual lives. Historically speaking, television has always been gay, and let us not forget that the original Mr. Television, Milton Berle, was a drag queen. And so from the Golden Age of the fifties to *The Golden Girls* of the eighties, there have always been hours and hours of fabulous escapist fare for the imaginative gay child. Which is not to say that we enjoyed everything equally. In fact, during those years when we had to watch TV with our families, we proclaimed our queerness by demanding to watch those shows that we, and nobody else, clamored to view. Until the early seventies, when most families had only one TV set, the most dreaded question we had to face was, "Just what the hell are you watching in there?"—the implication being that *The Dinah Shore Show* was not suitable fare for a nine-year-old male.

So what were the shows we loved the most? We have asked our friends their own favorites, and we've come up with a few choices ourselves. (One rule of thumb is that we liked shows in which the men wore tight pants and the women wore nice pants outfits.) In no particular order, then, we'd like to present our top-ten list of items that gay kids looked for when we perused *TV Guide:*

1. Situation comedies. It's been said that the average American child watches 20,000 hours of TV—and for the gay child, approximately 19,000 hours of this time were spent watching reruns of *Bewitched.* More than anything else, we gay children loved sailing through the channels looking for families with nice furniture and flattering lighting. Gay men love sitcoms so much that our subculture has been altered significantly by them. Nowadays, the average gay man's idea of a great "show tune" is more likely to be the credit sequence from *My Three Sons* than the overture from *My Fair Lady.*

2. Musical variety shows. Back in the fifties and sixties, we had shows that were actually based on talented performers rather than snazzy editing and computer graphics. Today, these musical shows look static, because when you had an Ella Fitzgerald or a Cyd Charisse performing, there was no need to splice cut. We even loved the less fabulous performers like the King Family, who had a Christmas show every year and relegated their less talented cousins to the background where they weren't allowed to sing. Other performers had their holiday shows, too, dreary older men like Don Ho and Perry Como whom our mothers seemed to find sexually attractive. And finally there were the fabulous nonentities like Claudine Longet, who appeared each year on the *Andy Williams Christmas Show,* giving new meaning to the carol "Silent Night" because she whispered so breathily we all thought the speakers on our TV sets had broken.

3. *Guest appearances by aging stars.* Every week we gay kids carefully searched *TV Guide* for possible appearances by the great stars from the Golden Age of Hollywood, such as Martha Raye, Claudette Colbert, Loretta Young, and Bette Davis, who were all playing their share of embarrassing cameos and supporting roles. Then there were those TV shows that seemed to specialize in giving great Hollywood broads their final chance to perform before the cameras—shows like *The Love Boat,* which guest-starred celebrities like Ethel Merman, Van Johnson, and Ann Miller.

4. *Campy comedians.* There have always been flamboyant actors on TV, people like Rip Taylor, Charles Nelson Reilly, and Alan Sues. In fact, as teenagers, we always suspected another kid was gay if he came to school quoting Paul Lynde's punchlines from *The Hollywood Squares.* In more recent times, Pee-Wee Herman confirmed what most of us felt in our hearts, that furniture was more fun to talk to than the straight adults in our lives. Imagine our shock when he was caught playing with himself—at a straight porn movie.

5. *TV characters who might have been gay.* In many shows there were characters who we found attractive and who showed no overt signs of heterosexuality. Robin, for instance, on *Batman* was a younger guy dependent on an older man, and had no girlfriends and no friends his own age. Ernie on *My Three Sons* was a shy kid adopted into a family of hunky teenage boys. And then there was John Boy Walton, the sensitive would-be writer in a large family that, according to statistics, must have had at least one queer. Many gay men report memories of their local weathermen seeming so queer that they half expected to hear the five-day forecast for Provincetown, even though they lived in Kansas City. And to this list we must add Bugs Bunny, who dressed up as Carmen Miranda and was always slapping big wet ones on Elmer Fudd. And finally there were those possible TV dykes—Miss Jane Hathaway, Kate Jackson's character on *Charlie's Angels*, Josephine the Plumber, and the Snoop Sisters.

6. *Actual gay characters.* Back in the seventies, a few queers finally did turn up on television. Unfortunately, they were like flowers that would bloom as gay for one season and then inexplicably come back the next season as straight. The worst of this lot was Billy Crystal on *Soap*, which started out cool when Jody came out of the closet, but then got cold feet when this character began dating women. The creators of this "breakthrough" show had the mistaken idea that a man could change his orientation as quickly as we gay viewers could change the channel to escape from this gutless piece of garbage. Then, in the eighties, *Dynasty* attempted this same ploy of pulling in the gay audience with a queer character and then turning the character around. Luckily for the producers of this soap opera, they had other gay male characters on board in the persons of the heavily painted Joan Collins, who looked like a shrunken negative of RuPaul, and the massively shoulder-padded Linda Evans, who would not have looked out of place playing tackle for the L.A. Rams.

TV writers in the nineties are smart enough to leave gay characters gay, though they do their best to make sure the characters are never seen enjoying themselves. Typically, gay characters are now seen hanging around straight people, giving them sage advice. Paraphrasing Arthur Bell (quoted in Vito Russo's *The Celluloid Closet*), gay men have become the new Mammies, updated versions of Hattie McDaniel. The best example of the nineties TV queer is the gay social worker on *Melrose Place*, who not only doesn't have much sex but also lacks a sense of humor. This is hardly an accurate representation, because any gay man will tell you that if you can't have one, you better have the other.

THREE'S A CROWD

Of all the television shows that have featured gay themes, none has done so quite as appallingly as the 1970s' hit *Three's Company*—the title referring to how infantile you'd have to be to enjoy such schlock. In this show, John Ritter (who had even less sex appeal than Thelma) was supposed to pretend to be gay in order to be allowed to live in a tacky apartment with two women, played by Suzanne Somers—that famous author, lecturer, and talk show hostess—and Joyce DeWitt. Not only did *Three's Company* reinforce the myth that being gay was a choice, it also suggested the absurd notion that any gay man might actually choose to live in an apartment with such cheap-looking furniture and hideous shag carpeting. Many parents could have effectively punished their gay children by forcing them to stay up late and watch this crap, which was equally insulting to straights.

7. *TV movies with gay themes.* After 1970, TV movies began to feature gay characters that were treated almost like real human beings. In the blink of an eye, we went from *Suddenly Last Summer* to *That Certain Summer*, a TV movie on ABC that dealt with a young boy who discovers that his father is gay. The problem with this film was that it starred Hal Holbrook as the father and Martin Sheen as his boyfriend. Yecch!! Even back then, one wouldn't have wanted to imagine these two men having any kind of sex, much less sex with each other. Their casting was all the more shocking considering that the gorgeous Jan Michael Vincent was probably hanging around doing nothing that year, and we would have much preferred seeing Jan laying a big wet one on Erik Estrada.

8. *Bad TV movies.* Even as kids, many of us were sophisticated enough to recognize bad acting and bad scripts, and mean enough to enjoy the sheer ineptness of minitalents like Linda Purl, Adrienne Barbeau, and Kim Darby trying to breathe life into TV movies in roles that would have defeated Meryl Streep. Back in the seventies, one string of these wretched vehicles kept Karen Black's career on life support a few years after it would have died a natural death. We authors most fondly remember *Trilogy of Terror*, in which the heroine was chased around her apartment by a one-foot-tall evil Zuni warrior doll, and the wonderfully clunky *The Girl Most Likely To*, written and directed by Joan Rivers and starring Stockard Channing, in which our heroine gets to live out every gay man's dream: She transforms herself through plastic surgery and then goes back to high school and murders all the perky kids who were mean to her before she got pretty.

9. *Funny women.* And, finally, we gay kids loved comediennes. In general, we have always found women much funnier than men. Let's face it, if queers ruled the airwaves, Phyllis Diller would be back in *The Pruitts of Southampton* immediately. Maybe we've always liked funny women best because they've always seemed to like us. Take Tracey Ullman, for example. Her brilliant sketches about a teenage girl being raised by her gay father are to *Saturday Night Live* what Shakespeare is to *Charles in Charge*. Then there's Roseanne, who never makes a big deal about the gay characters on her show. The high point of her career, in fact, was when she responded to Sandra Bernhardt's character's fear that coming out as a lesbian would ruin her relationship with the Conner family. Roseanne replied matter of factly, "Nah. We would have treated you like anyone else around here. We would have mocked you for a while—until we got tired of it and then we would have dropped it."

In the beginning, of course, there was only Lucille Ball, who was extraordinarily popular with gay men for three main reasons: In the original show her desperate attempts to break into show business, with absolutely no talent, paralleled the lives of half the gay men who wind up as career waiters in New York City. Secondly, her historic friendship with Vivian Vance provided a model for gay men, whose own friendships tend to be long-lasting and multifacted. And, finally, we got to enjoy the bittersweet melodrama of seeing this great star aging badly in public. Her voice dropped an octave. Her comic timing dropped out of sight. Her movies bombed, and she looked resentful and bitter on talk shows. But with every story we heard about her berating a costar or slapping a stewardess, we only loved Lucy all the more.

And, of course, there are women like Julia Child, who aren't technically comediennes but who have always been both gay-friendly and hilarious. Our favorite part of her show is its ending, when she invites her "friends" over to share what she has cooked. It always looks as if the producer simply went out on the street and grabbed the first ten boozy queens he could find and offered them dinner. In her own way, Julia Child has put more gay men on TV than anyone this side of Phil Donahue. But the funniest homo-friendly woman of all on television was probably Joan Rivers hosting *The Tonight Show* back in the early eighties. Her jokes about Elizabeth Taylor are still being quoted by gay men all over the world.

While we had our favorites, there were also shows that were guaranteed channel-skips for gay kids. Three categories that come to mind are:

1. Sports. Although this might be changing somewhat in the nineties, sports generally top our couldn't-care-less list. On Thanksgiving, while our fathers and brothers were in the living room watching the game, we were usually in the kitchen helping baste the turkey. And while they criticized some team's offensive strategy, we took issue with the half-time entertainment, which we usually found offensive. There were, however, several exceptions to the no-sports rule—men's swimming, gymnastics, and figure skating. In fact, we all look forward to the day when more of these athletes will dive, somersault, and figure eight out of the closet.

2. Westerns. In general—z-z-z-z-z-z. Not only were these shows taking place in dusty, unattractive neighborhoods, their production values were abysmal. Check out *Bonanza*. Anyone with an ounce of aesthetic sense could see that those backyard scenes were shot in a Burbank studio. You could all but spot the plastic trees labeled "Made in Korea." If we were forced to watch a Western, we much preferred *Wild, Wild West*, where every week the writers found another excuse to rip off hunky Robert Conrad's shirt and tie his hands behind his back.

3. *TV shows about World War II*. Puh-leez. Back in the early sixties, a rash of these dramas dotted the dial like hand grenade craters. Our male relatives were devoted fans and watched these wretched shows so often that the rest of the family should have gotten Veterans' benefits. We gay kids considered escaping to Canada rather than having to sit through another episode of Vic Morrow in *Combat*. When we got older, we began insisting on watching sitcoms instead and would sometimes compromise with *Hogan's Heroes*. Sad to say, we can still feel the long-term effects of these war shows—many of us still get horrifying flashbacks from John Wayne's performance in *The Green Berets* being shown on network TV.

THE CAROL BURNETT SHOW

Of all the TV women we loved, no one was funnier than Carol Burnett. When we were growing up she and her gang did the best TV sketches, and our personal favorites were probably the movie parodies. Everything we knew about the Golden Age of Hollywood we learned from this program. We all saw *Mildred Fierce* long before we ever saw *Mildred Pierce*, and it was Carol Burnett, not Gloria Swanson, who was our original Norma Desmond. And when we finally did get to see the MGM version of *Gone With the Wind,* we were all disappointed when Vivien Leigh didn't drape the curtains over her shoulders, curtain rod and all, and say, "I saw it in the window and I just had to have it." And when Carol mocked bad acting in a truly mediocre movie, like her classic send-up *Lovely Story,* she was even funnier, as when she indicated her eventual demise with demure little coughs: "uh-eh-uh-eh."

Carol also sent up soap operas with *As the Stomach Turns*, in which Vicki Lawrence, playing her long-lost daughter, would show up at her doorstep with an illegitimate baby and Carol would gush comically over the infant before casually throwing it in the umbrella stand. This sketch also had Harvey Korman's hilarious drag character, the stupendously buxom Mother Marcus, whose appearance onstage would always make Carol break character and crack up laughing. And, of course, there was the tragicomic Eunice, who had the most bracingly mean-spirited temper on television. This sketch was also fascinating because it gave Vicki Lawrence her first opportunity to display her talent for playing vicious old hags three times her actual age.

Whoever booked *The Carol Burnett Show*'s guest stars gave us the opportunity to see such camp luminaries as Mama Cass and Peggy Lee, not to mention the "illusionist" Jim Bailey actually doing full-drag impersonations of Judy and Barbra on network TV. And if all this wasn't enough, this show also offered the little gay kid a beefcake bonus in the frequently shirtless Lyle Wagonner, who was a major hunk in his day. In short, *The Carol Burnett Show* had more to offer the gay child than any other show on TV, and we were so glad to have that time together.

Chapter 16

Queer TV vs.
Non-queer TV

When we were growing up, there were TV shows that were queer, and there were TV shows that were not queer. But rather than try to explain these concepts theoretically, it would be easier to instruct by example. For instance, *Password*, hosted by the rather bland Allan Ludden, was non-queer, despite the fact that Mr. Ludden was married to perennial television diva Betty White. On the other hand, *The Hollywood Squares* with Paul Lynde deserves the highest "Q" rating of all (with the possible exception of the 1963 telecast of *The Judy Garland Show* in which Judy sang a duet with Barbra Streisand). A queer show was very simply a show that had an unquestionable gay resonance, and was one that gay men remember with affection, whereas a non-queer show was lacking in that certain *je ne sais queer*. Let's take a closer look at four pairs of television classics, each duo having much in common, except that one show was certifiably queer, while the other just didn't make the grade.

Example 1: *Bewitched* versus *I Dream of Jeannie*

We will begin by examining two situation comedies from the midsixties that shared the following premise: A woman who has extraordinary powers had to deny her magical abilities or risk losing the man she loved. In both shows the hero, in order to maintain his patriarchal privileges, kept the woman tucked safely out of sight. We're talking, of course, about *I Dream of Jeannie,* which we label non-queer, and *Bewitched,* which was just about the queerest comedy ever to play on network television.

What made *Jeannie* such a straight show? Part of it was the casting. Telegenic Barbara Eden apparently got the part more for her figure than for her ability to suggest emotional complexity, a ploy wasted on the young gay male. On the other hand, Larry Hagman, even during this early phase of his career, was starting to display the sour streak that, while it would later serve him well as a villain on *Dallas,* did nothing to make him charming in a light comedy. The supporting cast was unmemorable, and the plots, often revolving around the space program, were so tedious they made us want to slip some vodka into our Tang. This show was definitely a reaction to the burgeoning women's movement, and even as kids, we knew some-

thing was wrong and that the sensibility was already out of date.

The same could have been said
for *Bewitched*, except for one major
difference: The script writers most
often took the side of the deviants.
From the very beginning, this show
seemed to share the gay kid's point of view
that Samantha and her family were obviously wonderful people,
while Darren, the Tates,
and the Kravitzes were
selfish, humorless
straights who deserved
to be mocked. Beyond its
sensibility, *Bewitched* had a
queer subtext so obvious that a
Ph.D. thesis could be written on this
subject alone. Consider: The lead character
is, in effect, in the closet, and her husband is completely terrified
that anyone will discover that she's—gasp—a witch. What would
the boss think? What would the neighbors think? Most of all, what
would Darren's parents think? They could never handle the truth!
Sound familiar? Strangely enough, it was never really explained
just what would happen if Samantha's secret were let out, although
the implication was that she would undoubtedly be burned at the
stake.

And if the show's subtext was a perfect analogy to homophobia, the text was a blatant example of sexism. Darren was so
threatened by Samantha's powers that, in order for him to feel
emotionally secure, he forbade her from using her powers—not
even in the privacy of their own home! Instead of just twinkling
her nose and having the vacuum fast-forward its way around

the house, she had to do all the housework the hard way. The only time Darren condoned Samantha's witchcraft was when it was inevitably needed to save the day at the very last minute— which was why we were so delighted whenever Samantha got a chance to play her liberated cousin Sabrina, who would turn Darren into a donkey rather than put up with his tyranny.

Of course, what kept this situation from becoming dreary beyond belief was that Samantha had around her what most gay men eventually find—a supporting cast of cheerful eccentrics. Whereas Jeannie herself always seemed a little lonely in her bottle, Samantha had a mother more flamboyantly testy than any drag queen and more self-righteous than any activist—the wonderful Endora, brilliantly played by that great character actress Agnes Moorehead. As played by Maurice Evans, her father was a boozy bon vivant who would have seemed a familiar sight on any gay bar stool in the Western world. And who could forget Alice Ghostley as Esmerelda, Marian Lorne as Aunt Clara, and the ever-on-call Dr. Bombay? And then, of course, there was Paul Lynde as Uncle Arthur, who, along with that other great Arthur—Beatrice—had a voice and a delivery that were to comedy what lavender is to the color wheel. Lynde could take the most innocuous line of dialogue and give it a spin that made it gaily hilarious and slightly obscene. He even made his entrances with a certain innuendo, like the time that Samantha was vacuuming and a little sign came on the TV set instructing, "Pull knob." Samantha did so, and Paul Lynde's face appeared on the screen saying, "Oh, Sammy, you turn me on!"

What was crucial to this character's appeal was how Samantha herself reacted to Uncle Arthur. She—like her gay kid fans—obviously delighted in his eccentricities while having to conceal her giggles from Darren, who just as obviously hated this queen. Samantha's attitude toward Uncle Arthur mirrored that of gay viewers toward *Bewitched:* It was a guilty pleasure that we had to conceal from our families. And, of course, as time went on, the gay sensibility of this show became even more apparent. Ironically, Dick Sargent, the second actor to play Darren, came out as a gay man in the late eighties, and Elizabeth Montgomery has been a marshall in the Los Angeles Gay Pride Celebration. But the greatest tribute of all is how strongly gay kids still identify with the characters from *Bewitched*. One young man we know was so impressed with the Shakespearean authority with which Endora threw her spells, that when verbally abused by two bullies in the schoolyard, he replied, à la Agnes Moorehead, with his fingers twisting above his head—"Bat's wings, cow's eyes, the moon in eclipse!! Make them as effeminate as Quentin Crisp!" All in all, the success of this show was enough to make all gay kids want to wiggle their noses in triumph.

Example 2: *Green Acres* versus *Petticoat Junction*

Almost as bewitching as *Bewitched* was *Green Acres*, which we would like to label about as queer as you can get without being arrested in the state of Georgia. And in contrast to this we offer *Petticoat Junction*, which was set in the very same town of Hooterville, but, aside from the delightful Bea Benaderet, held absolutely no interest for us gay children. *Petticoat Junction* (which itself was spun off from *The Beverly Hillbillies*) was set in the Shady Rest boardinghouse, run by Aunt Kate; each week the Cannonball train would deposit a new guest whose job it was to start the dreary plots in motion. Other residents of the Shady Rest included Uncle Joe, a confirmed bachelor—we all had our doubts about him—and Kate's three buxom nieces, who collectively put the hooters in Hooterville. With all that cleavage hanging over the front porch, the plots were either sexist or dull, a typical one involving Uncle Joe's attempt to grow the biggest turnip in the county. In general, the dialogue from this show made *Hee-Haw* sound like George Bernard Shaw. Definitely N-Q.

Green Acres, on the other hand, went on the air a few years later, by which time the writers might as well have been using hallucinogenic drugs, judging by the increasingly preposterous plots and characters. The first episode began when Eddie Albert, as Oliver Douglas, left his Park Avenue apartment to pursue his lifelong dream of becoming a farmer, though subsequently he never managed to raise anything more than his eyebrows. He did, however, become the straight man for the most endearing mix of oddballs ever seen on mainstream TV.

Chief among these misfits was his wife, Lisa, played by Eva Gabor, who gamely attempted to be a housewife despite not having any domestic skills whatsoever. Her dinners were inedible, and rather than wash her dishes, she would just throw them out the window. Meanwhile, her shack of a home was eclectically decorated in sixties pop with elegant touches of Louis XIV (thus foreshadowing postmodernism by twenty years). Lisa likewise always seemed to be tripping on acid, as when she would "see" the opening credits and asked Oliver why there was writing in the house. Equally zonked were Mr. Haney, the junk salesman, and Mr. Kimble, the lunatic county extension agent. But, best of all were Alph, the carpenter, and his sister Ralph, who was an early dyke role model if there ever was one. Even more subversive were the Ziffels, played by two of the most repulsive character actors ever to work on network television, who were raising their "son" Arnold—a pig—who sat in front of the TV set watching the increasingly surreal plots unfold, such as the time UFOs landed, or the flashback to wartime Hungary when the Douglases first met.

The entire show was sublimely and unapologetically twisted: There we were, sitting in our houses, watching a pig watching the very same thing that we were watching. Was this the writers' way of commenting on the intelligence of the silent majority? In any event, *Green Acres* was definitely on our must-see list.

Example 3: *Lost in Space* versus *Star Trek*

Equally delightful—and equally Q—was *Lost in Space*, which, believe it or not, began its run as fairly serious science fiction and quickly evolved into intergalactic camp, due largely to that unsung hero, the totally fey Dr. Zachary Smith, played by Jonathan Harris. In the first episode, this dastardly villain was seen sneaking onto the Robinson family's spaceship. Was he a spy? A saboteur? Was he a desperate beautician trying to give June Lockhart a more flattering hairdo? Ms. Lockhart, the ultimate TV mom (*Lassie*), has actually admitted that after the third episode, *Lost in Space*'s writers "took the show in another direction." What an understatement! Gore Vidal himself might well have joined the writing staff, as Dr. Smith could not have been penned as being more effeminate if he'd been played by Zsa Zsa Gabor. He constantly bickered with the ship's robot, calling him a "Neanderthal ninny," or "bubble-headed booby," and whenever Don, the homophobic pilot of the ship, asked him to do any work, he would mince out of it, protesting, "My back is a disaster area!" He was such a queen that we half expected the robot to complain, "Danger, Will Robinson! Danger! If you're not careful you'll wind up like this big Mary!"

But at least this show *had* a queer character, which was more than we can say for *Star Trek*. Although groundbreaking in many ways, and a massive cult sensation, the show gets an ambivalent N-Q rating. We hesitate to definitively label this show as non-queer, as many gay men did love the program. If nothing else, it presented the future as an exciting time, and the starship *Enterprise* was a community where beings from every planet could work together in harmony. *Star Trek* was also groundbreaking in that it presented the first interracial kiss, between Captain Kirk and Lieutenant Uhuru, and Mr. Spock as the child of a human mother and a Vulcan father, which suggested a whole new universe of extraterrestrial sexual relationships.

Overall, though, the tone of this show was sanctimonious and square. The men—despite their stretch pants—lacked any sex appeal, and there was no character in *Star Trek* even remotely gay. (There was no excuse for this oversight, especially since the capital of the United Federation of Planets was in San Francisco.) Wouldn't it have been fabulous if a gay male character snapped opened his communicator one day and used it as a compact? Why couldn't they have pulled Paul Lynde off the set of *Bewitched* to play a crew member? We can just hear him calling out, "Beam me up, Scotty, and while you're at it, take ten pounds off my hips!" Speaking of which, were we the only ones who noticed that Captain Kirk, played by William Shatner, looked more and more like the planet Jupiter as the series progressed?

In the final analysis, we should probably just give *Star Trek* a lower-case *q*, if only for its campy sixties miniskirted costumes, go-go boots, and beehive hairdos. We particularly enjoyed the makeup on all the alien woman, who, in order to suggest otherworldliness, boldly wore eyeliner where no eyeliner had ever gone before!

Example 4: *Batman* versus *Superman*

As we've suggested, one of the sure signs that a TV series is dominated by a straight male sensibility is when it offers as a sex symbol some slob most gay men wouldn't look at twice. For this reason alone we have decided to pass judgment on the old *Superman* series starring George Reeves and give it a decisive N-Q rating. Not to be unfair to Mr. Reeves, but come on! How could you call a guy who was so obviously out of shape Superman? That big "S" on this Superman's costume could have stood for "snacking." This was a Man of Steel who never missed a meal: The easiest way Lex Luthor could have killed him was by giving him a box of kryptonite donuts. Sad to say, George Reeves was light-years away from the adorable Dean Cain, who played Superman in the 1993 television series *Lois and Clark*. (The only interesting appearance that George Reeves ever made as Superman was on an episode of *I Love Lucy*, when he came to visit for little Ricky's birthday. What the writers of this show didn't reveal was Superman's real motivation in coming to the party—which was an opportunity to chow down on some birthday cake.) In short, Superman's boxy physique, bulked up, but devoid of muscle tone, was an insult to every all-American gay boy who, each week, would hold his comic book up to the TV screen, compare physiques, and sigh, "What a porker!"

Now, Adam West as the Q-rated Batman may also have been on the pudgy side, but that was okay, because his character was always played for laughs. *Batman* turned into a complete gay hoot in the mid-sixties because, before *The Love Boat* set sail, it was the one program where we could always expect to see our favorite Hollywood has-beens. Any show that managed to create juicy roles for Ethel Merman, Tallulah Bankhead, and Victor Buono had to be okay in our book, and to this day catfights are still breaking out in gay bars over who made the best Catwoman—Julie Newmar, Lee Merriweather, or Eartha Kitt.

Example 5: *The Mary Tyler Moore Show*

While there are other television shows we could talk about—we loved *The Addams Family*, which was gay enough to provide the basis for two Paul Rudnick screenplays, and hated *Family Affair*, which was syrupy enough to give Aunt Jemima diabetes—but one series was our absolute favorite, and so we'd like to end our chapter on a high note by inducting *The Mary Tyler Moore Show* into our Queer TV Hall of Fame. When the all-Mary cable network is created—our version of MTV—you can bet that every gay man in America will be glued to his set. Mary was our prime role model. (In fact, one decorator queen we know doesn't consider a room finished until he's hung a great big "M" on the wall.) Here was a single woman, in an urban setting, working in a creative field. Here was a gal who dated a lot of guys, had a loving biological family, and yet was mainly committed to her friends. And Mary's friends were all people you'd definitely want to hang out with: There was man-hungry Rhoda and narcissistic Phyllis. At work there was Murray with his bitchy remarks, topped only by the cheerfully sexcrazed Sue Ann Nivens. Georgette was a refreshing take on the dizzy blonde, and even the straight men in the cast, Ted Baxter and Lou Grant, had charm and vulnerability. Best of all, each character had a warm and rounded relationship with Mary herself, and so as gay children we always knew that—even though our lives would be different—we were going to make it after all.

ONLY *WE* KNEW THAT...

Gay fans of *Star Trek* know trivia about this show that straight fans would never even consider. First and foremost, *Star Trek* was produced by Desilu Studios, and was originally okay'd for production by Lucille Ball herself. Now, Ms. Ball, no fan of science fiction, had to be told the difference between "UFO shows" and "USO shows," because she originally thought the title of the series referred to Hollywood stars being dragged around the world to entertain the troops. We're just thankful that Lucy didn't guest star on an episode, which would no doubt have involved her screwing up the transporter and beaming Captain Kirk to the wrong planet, where he might have run into Jack Benny doing a cameo as a Klingon.

Chapter 17

The Gay Episodes

The TV phenomenon that most changed the expectations of young queer America was "the gay episode": a single show in an otherwise straight series that explored the different ways in which the theme of homosexuality could be introduced into the lives of the regular characters. The following two examples are exemplary, in that they were well intentioned, well produced, and followed the three basic rules of good gay comedy:

1. They treated their gay characters matter of factly.

2. They were genuinely funny.

3. Unlike this book, they didn't exploit stereotypes.

The first example is the *All in the Family* episode in which Mike and Gloria had a flamboyantly gay friend, who appalled the homophobic Archie. Luckily, the writers for this show had an interesting plot twist when Archie, who had been making homophobic remarks about this character down at the local bar, discovered that a football player he respected—and who had just beaten him at arm wrestling—was also gay. Archie, needless to say, was stunned. As was Phyllis on *The Mary Tyler Moore Show* when she found out that her brother was gay. This news was broken to her by Rhoda, to whom the brother had become attached—which alone should have tipped Phyllis off. Rhoda, you see, was one of those women, exemplified by Elizabeth Taylor, to whom gay men are attracted as surely as a compass points true north.

While both of these gay episodes appeared post-Stonewall, wouldn't it have been great if some of the shows of the fifties and sixties that we grew up with had produced gay shows as well? What would they have been like?

1. I Love Lucy. Star-struck Lucy, who is in Hollywood in search of celebrities, overhears Rock Hudson trying to pick up a waiter at the Brown Derby. She wants to meet Rock herself, so, after convincing a reluctant Ethel, the two women disguise themselves in black leather hats and jackets and go cruising on Santa Monica Boulevard. Lucy and Ethel are soon in heaven because in the first gay bar they enter are all their favorite actors: James Dean, Montgomery Clift, Danny Kaye, Laurence Olivier, and Sal Mineo. The girls are forced to make a hasty retreat, though, when Charles Laughton tries to hit on Ethel.

2. The Honeymooners. Alice has a gay brother who visits the Kramdens and is mortified when he sees how Alice is living. Against Ralph's wishes they go to Gimbels and finally buy some curtains for the apartment.

3. Make Room for Daddy. Danny starts wearing leather harnesses around the house and demanding that everyone call him "sir." His friends and family all become submissive, except for Pat Carroll, who just goes on acting like herself.

4. *Queen for a Day*. Liberace turns up on the show and, before he even opens his mouth, the applause meter goes wild.

5. *This Is Your Life*. For a special episode called *This Is Your Real Life*, Ralph Edwards outs a famous Hollywood closet case by bringing onto the stage the busboy the celebrity fondled at Caesar's Palace back in 1957 and who is now working for the LAPD.

6. *The Dick Van Dyke Show*. The man-hungry Sally becomes girl-hungry, and, taking the bow out of her hair, tries to steal Pickles away from Buddy. Meanwhile, Mel waxes his entire body, leaving Buddy free to make bald jokes about parts of Mel's torso that nobody has ever seen before.

7. *Bonanza*. Hoss and Little Joe turn the Ponderosa into a country-western bar featuring two-stepping on Tuesday nights.

8. *The Judy Garland Show*. This series was so gay that it needed to have a straight episode: Judy chats with former heavyweight champion Sonny Liston, who hums "The Ballad of the Green Berets."

9. *Dragnet*. Gannon and Friday go to New York City to help control the Stonewall riots, where two transvestites beat the hell out of them for being so boring.

10. *The Beverly Hillbillies*. Granny joins SAGE—Senior Action in a Gay Environment—on the mistaken notion that she will be able to obtain the herb for her possum stew.

11. The Andy Griffith Show. Floyd changes his name to Mr. Floyd, becomes a stylist, and gives Aunt Bea a complete beauty makeover. This leads Opie to ask Andy some embarrassing questions, and that night Andy tells his son that the town of Mayberry was actually named after a drag queen—May Berry—who was its original settler.

12. Batman. Paul Lynde guest stars as Catty Man, who's disrupting Gotham City with his scathing remarks. He captures the Dynamic Duo and turns them into a Thrilling Threesome by tying up Robin and making Batman watch as he spanks him. Smack!!! Pow!!! Wham!!!

13. Gilligan's Island. The Skipper finally reveals that he and Gilligan have been sharing the same hammock for years. Trouble soon brews between Mr. Howell and the Skipper, who has now begun to openly call his "little buddy" "lovey."

14. My Three Sons, Family Affair, Petticoat Junction, and Hazel. Back in the sixties and early seventies, it was common to see characters jumping from one sitcom to another, such as *Maude*, who was spun off from *All in the Family.* Here, then, is the supreme gay episode that we would have loved to have seen: Two middle-aged male housekeepers, Uncle Charlie and Mr. French, decide "to hell with the kids" and run off together to Key West, where they open a bed and breakfast. Next door to them is their old friend Hazel, who has finally told Mr. B to clean up after himself. Hazel is now busy building Sappho's Inn with Aunt Kate, who has given up the Shady Rest and moved South. In a sweet reunion, these four old friends sit around a pool and give thanks that they can finally be themselves.

THE UNINTENTIONAL GAY EPISODE

Some TV shows had gay episodes without even realizing it. A good example occurred in *The Lucy Show* episode in which Ethel Merman was the guest star. These two aging show-biz divas were such a sight in white pancake and rouged lips that anyone who tuned in by accident might have thought they were watching Kabuki. But what made this show so gay was that the story began with Lucy's eight-year-old son begging her to get Ethel Merman to star in a show to raise money for his Cub Scout troop: Apparently, all the boys in the troop just loved Ethel Merman, and they had all her records. What kind of troop *was* this? Were they all working for merit badges in musical theater? It seemed obvious to us that this was one TV kid who never would have given Lucy grandkids for her last show.

Chapter 18

And Now a Word from Our Sponsor

Recently, Ikea made national news by airing a commercial in which, for the first time ever, two gay men were seen shopping for the home they clearly shared, picking out a dining room table. While we applaud the effort, the premise is a little ridiculous: What gay men could ever make this decision in only sixty seconds? A purchase like this would require nothing less than a miniseries. Nevertheless, we look forward to more gay commercials, ideally featuring such gay spokespersons as Melissa Etheridge for Purina Cat Chow, Sir Ian McKellen for Geritol, and, finally, RuPaul for Cover Girl. We would also love to see a gay commercial for Excedrin. Why not have a young queer flipping channels late at night. He would come across Pat Robertson in the *700 Club* and then reach into the medicine cabinet as the announcer intones, "Homophobia got you down?"

In the meantime, we must content ourselves with commercials that, while not explicitly gay, are pretty homoerotic. From the Marlboro man through Marky Mark, certain ads look as if they were invented by horny gay men. We mean, who wrote that commercial for Diet Coke in which a man's bare chest stops work in an office four stories above his head? Although many straight people were upset by this ad's depiction of lusty female office workers drooling at their window, we thought it awfully tame. Gay kids have been eroticizing a number of icons of American advertising for years. The major object of our fantasies has been Mr. Clean, who, with a hard body, earring, and housekeeping skills was great marriage material. The next most popular was the Jolly Green Giant, who had great legs, wore a tight miniskirt made of broccoli, and had us all singing, "In the valley of the jolly ho-ho-ho mosexual!"

We gay kids also loved those commercials featuring wise-cracking women like Madge the Manicurist for Palmolive Dishwashing liquid, who soaked her clients' hands in liquid detergent while gleefully insulting them, a sort of cross between Betty Crocker and the Marquis de Sade. Even more fun was the way that television commercials kept our favorite actresses in front of the cameras decades after any studio would ever bankroll a movie starring them. Once again we surveyed our friends for their favorites, and we present our collective Hall of Fame:

1. Phyllis Diller for Snowy Bleach. "This stuff is so good it can even get the yellow out of my birth certificate! A-ha-ha-ha-ha-haaaaaaa!"

2. Ann Miller for Great American Soups. She did her own version of the cancan by strapping on a can and then tapping away on the top of one.

3. Ethel Merman for Liquid Vel dishwashing detergent. As she sang, the camera panned up from her kitchen sink, and we saw that she was on a set of a Broadway show! She sang "Honey, everything's coming up roses, try Vel and you'll seeeeeeeeeee!" What made this commercial even more hilarious was that we *knew* that Ethel Merman had never washed a dish in her life.

4. Coffee Commercials. By far the most fertile format for jump-starting old careers was the coffee ad. First we had Vivian Vance pushing a coffee cart for Maxwell House, and then we had Margaret Hamilton as Cora the town busybody who was always brewing up a fresh pot. In general, mature actresses with scotch-whiskey voices were preferred for this genre, as though they couldn't be considered appropriate pitchwomen for java unless their delivery was more sepulchral than James Earl Jones's. First we had the only recently recovered Patricia Neal for Maxim Coffee drawling, "Wh-en m-ah-y huh-sband co-mes ho-me frah-m a ha-a-ard da-y at the office ..." Then, a few years later, we had the completely unconvincing Lauren Bacall for High Point Coffee barking, "Aaaah, The flavor!" Ms. Bacall always sounded so haughty in this role that, if you actually gave her a cup of that instant brew, she'd toss it right back in your face.

Chapter 19

The Birth of a Queer Nation

or, How We Learned to Love the Movies

t almost goes without saying that gay men adore great films and that we take them very seriously. Academy Award night is for gay men what Super Bowl Sunday is for straights: We invariably gather in front of our TV sets, snack guiltlessly, and knowledgeably discuss the statistics. We announce things like, "Katharine Hepburn leads the league with four wins, followed by Walter Brennan with three, closely followed by Bette Davis, Spencer Tracy, and Jodie Foster with two apiece." Also, like straight men, we're very likely to leap from our seats and scream angrily at the TV screen. The only difference is that while straight men might feel outraged over a missed pass, we're more likely to be howling in anguish over Kim Basinger's dress. We're undoubtedly the greatest critics, fans, and connoisseurs of the silver screen. The question is: How did we get this way?

The more we thought about this question, the more we became convinced that (for Baby Boomers and Generation Xers, in any case) our uniquely queer appreciation of movies

actually developed much more slowly than our love of television. For one thing, cinema was such a magical medium that
the mere experience of going to the movies often overshadowed
the quality of the film itself. For another, most of the really
great movies, which have long since become the lingua franca
of the gay community, came out of a Golden Age of Hollywood
that had ended long before we were born, and so we didn't even
see these films until years later, when we first began frequent-
ing art houses and the classic film section of Blockbuster
Video.

But to begin with, the actual physical experience of going to
the movies simply overwhelmed our senses, and so the medium
far outweighed the message. We were so taken in by the bright-
ness of the colors and the size of the screen that even the
cheesiest *Planet of the Apes* movie could seem like a masterpiece. When watching television we were merely turning our
backs on reality, but going to movie theaters meant that we'd
escaped reality completely. For children, these auditoriums
were colossal adult spaces, and we were all too conscious of
having entered a mysterious temple built on a grand scale.
Going to the movies also meant that we'd be treated with the
respect due a paying customer, so there was no danger that our
father would try to remove us from his chair, or that our mother
would ask us to lift our feet while she vaccuumed. We'd be able
to buy snacks totally unlike anything our mom kept at home in
the fridge: candies like Sno-Caps, Raisinets, jawbreakers, and
Goobers. Years later we're much more likely to recall the taste
of Jujuby's than the plot of *Born Free*.

If a gay film aesthetic took time to develop it was also due to
the fact that we simply didn't see that many movies. Unlike
television, wherein we chose what we wanted to watch on an
hourly basis, going to the movies was a special occasion. So our
idiosyncratic viewing habits weren't apparent from the start.

For us sophisticates currently living in urban centers who taxi to the Cineplex at the drop of a hat, it's humbling to remember that we haven't always been so erudite. In fact, there was actually a time when we couldn't tell the difference between *The Ghost and Mrs. Muir* and *The Ghost and Mr. Chicken;* when Don Knotts may very well have seemed like the epitome of great film acting.

This isn't to say that the seeds weren't being planted for what would later blossom into a full-blown gay sensibility. Concurrent with these early experiences at our local cinemas, we were slowly becoming aware of filmdom's more glorious past, often while we were watching television. It was probably some rainy afternoon in front of the TV set when we first became transfixed while watching *Humoresque* with Joan Crawford, or *Niagara* with Marilyn Monroe. Then maybe there was that Friday evening when the babysitter fell asleep and we got to watch *The Late Show* featuring *Camille*, with some amazing woman named Greta Garbo. And, of course there was the yearly broadcast of *The Wizard of Oz*, which for young gays was a Rosetta Stone, unlocking the secrets of an earlier culture which had flowered long before we were born. We didn't just watch this movie; we studied it for clues about the life of Judy Garland and the advent of MGM musicals. If nothing else *The Wizard of Oz*, made in 1939, was the first classic film we loved, so it gave us our initial opportunity to complain, "They don't make them like that anymore!"

Television wasn't the only means by which we were going back to our futures. If we were lucky enough to have film buffs for mothers, old *Photoplay* magazines could be dug out of the attic with articles about Jean Arthur and Myrna Loy. As we grew older, we began sneaking into the adult library and discovering the guilty pleasure of hiding behind the stacks and reading whole *books* about women like Marlene Dietrich and

Vivien Leigh. And then there were those stories, recounted over coffee and cake, about how members of our very own families had brushed up against movie stars, like the time Aunt Grace had seen Claudette Colbert getting gas at the Sinclair Station, or the day Irene Dunne had stepped on Aunt Sylvia's toe at a matinee of *My Sister Eileen.*

Meanwhile, some of these great ladies were actually still making movies, although their stock in Hollywood had dropped precipitously. In the early sixties *Whatever Happened to Baby Jane?* was spawning a whole new horror genre in which Bette, Joan, and Olivia were scaring the pants off us by appearing onscreen without makeup in movies such as *The Nanny, I Saw What You Did, and I Know Who You Are,* and *Lady in a Cage.* As gay kids we had just discovered who these women were and, while our brothers were hankering to see *Night of the Living Dead,* we were the only boys on the block willing to fork over our allowance for *Die! Die! My Darling!* with Tallulah Bankhead.

This may have been the turning point.

For many of us, there was a moment when we discovered that our taste in movies had mysteriously turned unconventional. Until we were perhaps nine or ten, we'd been going along with the crowd, but after the turning point we began going to the movies alone and lying about what we'd seen. How many of us remember our mothers dropping us off at the local Twinplex for a "boy's movie" like *Journey to the Center of the Earth* and then sneaking next door to watch a "woman's movie" like *The Wheeler Dealers,* a bedroom farce starring Lee Remick? The worst part came two hours later, trying to explain to our mother why we were coming out of the theater fifteen minutes later than scheduled.

And then something even more miraculous occurred: We went through puberty, and going to the movies took on a whole new meaning. Once the hormones kicked in, the dream factory became a wet-dream factory. From the bad boy movies of the fifties through the surfer boy movies of the sixties, we were now running to films like *Rebel Without a Cause, Splendor in the Grass,* and *Beach Blanket Bingo.* In addition to Bette and Judy, our new idols were James Dean, Warren Beatty, and Frankie Avalon. We wanted to be *Where the Boys Are.* We all had our favorites, and the magnitude of their beauty on the silver screen beat anything found on television. Men like Troy Donahue, Tab Hunter, Steve McQueen, and Paul Newman all made us so hot that we could have made popcorn on our laps. Then *A Hard Day's Night* opened, and all the other actors were forgotten: There was only Paul.

Thus, by the time we graduated high school, the two main pillars supporting the gay film aesthetic were firmly in place: a sweet nostalgia for a more glamourous past, coupled with an insistent hankering for the current box office hunk. From this point on films were less of an escape from reality and more of an escape into our own private world. In other words, some time between queer childhood and queer adulthood movie theaters became magical places where we went to sit in the dark and finally be ourselves, and it's been like that ever since.

As we've shown, there comes a turning point where gays and straights develop very different tastes in movies. Whereas straight boys flock to movies like *The Babe Ruth Story*, in which life is lived on a baseball field, gay boys eventually find movies like *All About Eve*, where all the world's a stage. The following series of contrasts will help to drive this point further into the ground, and guide you in classifying Queer and Non-Queer films.

Straight boys like movies where the bad guy loses.
Gay boys like movies where the bad girl wins.

Straight boys like movies with dog fights.
Gay boys like movies with catfights.

Straight boys like movies where cars blow up.
Gay boys like movies where relationships blow up.

Straight boys like movies with toga parties.
Gay boys like movies with cocktail parties.

Straight boys like movies with baseball diamonds.
Gay boys like movies where diamonds are a girl's best
   friend.

Straight boys want to be as tough as Humphrey Bogart.
Gay boys want to be as tough as Lauren Bacall.

Straight boys remember the *Maine.*
Gay boys remember Marjorie Main.

Straight boys like *How the West Was Won.*
Gay boys like *West Side Story.*

Straight boys like *The Magnificent Seven.*
Gay boys like *Seven Brides for Seven Brother.*

Chapter 20

The Good, the Bad, and the Nutty Professor

What were the films we were most likely to have seen as kids, and how did we feel about them? Until a certain point in our lives, gays often saw the same movies as everyone else, but as with mainstream TV, we didn't always watch them in quite the same way as our peers. For instance, that strong and silent Western hero, whose reticence may have been perceived as a virtue by all the other guys, merely looked to us like some big lug avoiding intimacy. On that dissenting note, here are some brief notes on a few other genres:

Fantasies: As a rule, gay men enjoyed fantasy movies made specifically for children, but we tended to forget them rather quickly. They've long since blurred in our minds into something like *That Darn, Shaggy, Absent-Minded Love Bug,* in which Dean Jones, Kurt Russell, or Tommy Kirk was upstaged by a devious household pet or a talking means of transportation. In general, gay kids weren't really innocent enough to fully appreciate such whimsy. We also had mixed feelings about films in which happy families lived and worked together. Thus a movie like *Swiss Family Robinson*, in which some children were shipwrecked with their parents in a tropical treehouse, was about as disturbing to us as *The Diary of Anne Frank* with coconuts.

On the other hand, many of us were fascinated by those bizarre movies in which a socially maladjusted boy preferred to converse with a chimpanzee, a dolphin, or a dog in such films as *Toby Tyler*, *Old Yeller*, and *Flipper*. Unfortunately, the mammal in question was invariably wiser than the young Homo sapien, and generally a much better actor, so we found it difficult to believe in bright futures for these kids other than as cage cleaners or dog walkers. In retrospect, these simpleminded films, featuring inappropriate pets such as ferrets, grizzly bears, and raccoons, were just a short leap to a horror movie like *Willard* in which our young sociopath befriends some rats and uses them to kill Ernest Borgnine.

Cartoon features: The most memorable characters from these films are nearly always the villains, and our all-time favorite was Cruella De Vil from *101 Dalmations*. Until *Mommie Dearest*, this lethal fur fancier was the closest thing we had to the real Joan Crawford. We also loved Snow White's evil stepmother and Maleficent from *Sleeping Beauty*. These women were so stylish and witty that we could forgive them for wanting to destroy their relatives, kind of like evil Anti Mames. As for the current crop of Disney films, we predict that Gaston, that narcissistic muscle queen from *Beauty and the Beast*, will be talked about at cocktail parties long after Aladdin has faded from memory.

Mythology movies: This genre featured characters like Sinbad, Jason, and Thor, and generally took place during a time in history when Ray Harryhausen monsters walked the earth. Therefore, the villain in these flicks was usually a Cyclops the size of the Chrysler building, who walked so slowly that he could be easily outrun by the hero. Other popular antagonists in such films were seven-headed Hydras, evil Medusas, and assorted dragons who, although supposedly invincible, were easily dispatched by the hero, who generally knew just where to stab them. Although hokey and unconvincing, these flicks were often among our favorites. In addition to educating us about the pagan roots of Western civilization, they were fabulous excuses to have lots of hunky men running around wearing nothing more than the skins of animals they'd killed in the previous scenes.

The best examples of this genre were undeniably the Hercules movies that poured out of Italy during the fifties and sixties. Even the posters for these features were exciting, as they generally pictured a giant Hercules towering above the titles with a chest so expanded that iron chains were bursting, along with our hearts. These films were also significant to gay children because they were our first exposure to leather harnesses, bicep bracelets, and bad lipsynching. In addition, they revolutionized Hollywood standards of male beauty. Until this time, movie musculature was a rarity, and one could have been considered a hunk by merely taking off one's shirt without assistance. Steve Reeves, a former Mr. Universe, changed all that, and nowadays even the likes of Kenneth Branagh are working out their pecs before stepping in front of the camera.

Science Fiction: The best parts of sci-fi films were when some pompous jerk would suddenly lose his temper, try to kill a radioactive ant with a pistol, and then get pulled off the ground kicking and screaming. Another glorious moment was when some giant reptile would stomp carelessly through a suburban neighborhood, swatting station wagons off the highway with his tail, and burning the roofs off houses every time he belched. In short, from *Godzilla* and *The Blob,* gay kids in the fifties got to see their revenge fantasies played out on the grandest scale possible. Our sympathies were rarely for the straight society being destroyed but rather for the alien monster itself, who never really frightened us as he was meant to. Years later, when *Star Wars* opened, we experienced a similar phenomenon: Rather than being terrified by Darth Vader or Jabba the Hut, we didn't scream out in horror until we saw Carrie Fisher's ridiculous hairdo, at which point many of us fainted and had to be carried from the theater.

Horror Films: Likewise, classic horror films such as *Dracula* have long had a fascination for gay kids. What could be queerer than an elegant man who wears a cape, sleeps all day, and can be warded off by garlic and the wrong jewelry? The Wolfman also had gay undertones, as it featured a guy who goes out at night and turns into an animal. Not surprisingly, one of the earliest directors of horror films, James Whale, was an openly gay filmmaker, and his two classics, *Frankenstein* and *The Bride of Frankenstein,* have many queer elements. In the former, a misunderstood offspring is rejected by his creator and spends the rest of the movie awkwardly searching for love. In the latter a woman with a punk hairdo screams out in horror at being forced into an unwanted heterosexual coupling.

Steven Spielberg, one of the best directors of modern horror films, has terrified his audiences with monsters as diverse as a great white shark in *Jaws,* a Tyrannosaurus rex in *Jurassic Park,* and, most frightening of all, Joan Crawford at the end of her career in *Night Gallery.* Crawford herself is the subject of what is probably the gay horror flick par excellence, *Mommie Dearest.* When Faye Dunaway as Joan Crawford screeches, "No more wire hangers!" it's like a Household Hint from Hell-oise. If nothing else, Faye Dunaway's brilliant impersonation of Ms. Crawford was frighteningly accurate. In fact, we believe that she would have received much more acclaim if only the script hadn't been so preposterous. Instead her ghoulish portrayal sank her career as certainly as an iceberg sank the *Titanic*— which just goes to point out the tragedy of what happens when bad movies happen to fairly good actresses.

Christmas movies: Many of these films, which were shown on television every year, weren't nearly so inspiring as *The Wizard of Oz*. In fact, several of them left us out in the winter cold completely. One such film was Frank Capra's *It's a Wonderful Life*, starring Jimmy Stewart and Donna Reed. This ambitious movie is the story of a small-town hero, George Bailey, who's given the chance to learn what the world would have been like if he'd never been born. In the movie's pivotal scene, the sleepy, idyllic town of Bedford Falls is transformed into the garish Pottersville, and we see George Bailey running down the main street past smoky honky-tonks and strip joints with neon signs screaming GIRLS! GIRLS! GIRLS! Meanwhile, the background music blares jazzily to underscore how horrifying Pottersville has become. As George stumbles through his nightmare landscape he encounters Violet, the bad girl in town, being thrown into a paddy wagon screaming at a cop, "I know every big shot in this town. I know Potter himself!"

Now, the big problem for queer kids was that Mr. Capra seemed to be saying that this town was evil merely for having a little nightlife. In reality, most of us spent our childhoods dreaming of escaping from boring towns like Bedford Falls, with the hope of one day finding a city like Pottersville where we might actually meet someone. It's not that all gay men hate sleepy little towns, which are often swell places to go antiquing or to buy a summer home, but very few of us would want to live there year round. And speaking of buying homes, another Christmas classic that was somewhat of a stretch for literal-minded gay kids was *Miracle on 34th Street.* This was the story of a little girl, played by Natalie Wood, who had the nerve to ask Kris Kringle to buy her a house for Christmas. What a spoiled brat. What would she want the following year? Commercial real estate? They might as well have called this one *The Leona Helmsley Story,* for rarely has such capitalistic greed been so unconsciously sentimentalized in a mainstream Hollywood flick.

Sports Movies: As we've indicated, gay boys responded to movies about sports a lot differently than straights. *Field of Dreams,* to pick a recent example, left straight boys cheering and gay boys wanting to run screaming from the theater. In this dopey film, the All-American pastime was a cosmic metaphor, and Heaven was a place where grown men were forced to play baseball constantly. Most gay men would rather spend their afterlives in Dante's Inferno than be stuck in right field, where we'd be dropping flyballs for eternity. A subset of this genre involved some poor athlete's coming down with a terminal disease. In films like *Pride of the Yankees, Brian's Song,* and *Bang the Drum Slowly,* youthful triumphs were followed by emotional bonding, alarming early symptoms, courageous struggles, and the inevitable ascension into heaven. For some reason, our fathers and brothers, who would have scoffed at our sobbing over *Dark Victory,* got all misty-eyed over these flicks. For them the loss of life was sad, but the loss of a possible World Series–winning team was an excruciating tragedy.

Of course we gay boys did have one emotional response in common with the straight men in our families: We all hated to see animals die, and we left the movies sobbing whenever a boy's best friend passed on to his doggie reward. This leads us to believe that the most successful sports tearjerker, one that would have both gay and straight appeal, has yet to be made— the story of a sick and dying animal athlete. For instance, it could be the story of a greyhound whose brilliant racing career is cut short by terminal distemper.

Slapstick comedy: Our general dislike for competitive sports also affected our appreciation of at least one classic comedy routine, Abbott and Costello's "Who's on First?" To our thinking, they should have just called this bit "Who Cares Who's on First?" But while we didn't share our culture's fascination with baseball, we were certainly intrigued by the fact that, in their films, these two men lived together, worked together, and hung out with the Andrews Sisters. Then, again, many slapstick comedies had homoerotic subtexts. Why, for instance, did so many comedy teams have to sleep in the same bed? George Burns and Gracie Allen were legally married, but the Three Stooges had no such excuse. If these guys ever had a commitment ceremony, we never saw it. The trio was forever poking at each other, grunting at each other, and removing each other's hair. In fact, one might argue that Moe, Larry, and Curly were practicing safe sex long before anyone else.

War movies: After seeing a film like *The Longest Day*, most gay kids would agree that this seemingly endless flick more than deserved its name. These noisy movies, featuring reluctant male bonding under the most dire of circumstances, were simply overwrought, repetitious, and grim. Also, what good was casting hunks like Marlon Brando or Rod Taylor if you were then going to hide them in baggy uniforms and roll them around in the mud? The only good thing about these films was that many of them took place in exotic locations like the South

Pacific, Italy, and France, although we could have easily imagined far more pleasant ways of visiting these places than having to wade ashore under heavy artillery.

There was, however, one delightful subset of war movies—war musicals, featuring stars like Betty Grable, Danny Kaye, and Dinah Shore, who risked their lives in order to sing show tunes to the troops. Most recently, Bette Midler tried to revive war musicals with her major flop *For the Boys*, which might as well have been called *For the Gay Boys*, as most straight audiences ignored this movie completely. We are greatly saddened by the loss of this genre and would someday like to make our own contribution to it. In our film all those cute young soldiers would get to stay home while criminally untalented performers like Donny Osmond and Brooke Shields would be issued machine guns and forced to fight in the trenches.

Disaster movies: Our final genre applies to those of us who were still kids in the seventies. This was a short-lived series of films in which Hollywood filmmakers tried to devise as many catastrophes as possible to kill off an earlier generation of Hollywood icons. In movies such as *Airport*, *Earthquake*, and *The Towering Inferno* we gay kids were horrified to see such venerable performers as Helen Hayes, Ava Gardner, and Fred Astaire being blown up, smothered, and fried. This genre did have its rewards though, like the time Shelley Winters had to dog paddle for her life in *The Poseidon Adventure*. In one brief scene Ms. Winters became the most famous swimmer in film since Esther Williams.

Chapter 21

A Co-star Is Born

Whenever a gay man comes out to his friends or co-workers, he is generally asked three stupid questions:

1. Why did you choose to be gay?

2. Why do you wear an earring in your left ear?

3. Why do you guys like Bette Davis so much?

Our fascination with Hollywood actresses is well known, and one could stroll into any gay bookstore in the world, and the most shelf space would be devoted to movie star bios, from the irrepressibly tough Barbara Stanwyck to the horribly tragic Rita Hayworth. Nobody can fully explain this phenomenon. Maybe we're searching for the mothers we never had, or maybe we're contemplating, with horror, images of the mothers we *did* have.

Who knows? The answer is probably "all of the above," or even, "none of the above" because, believe it or not, there are actually some gay men who care very little about movie actresses and wouldn't know the difference between Sid Caesar and Cyd Charisse.

On the average, however, gay men are the preeminent fans of all the great ladies. We could tell you not only what actresses played what parts but also what actresses were considered for roles that were later given to somebody else. We know, for instance, that Shirley Temple was originally supposed to play Dorothy Gale, Claudette Colbert was first slated for the role of Margo Channing, and that Doris Day was the director's first choice for Mrs. Robinson. We could tell you why Lena Horne was passed over for the role of Magnolia. We could tell you how Marni Nixon dubbed the singing voices of Deborah Kerr, Natalie Wood, and Audrey Hepburn. We could even tell you what the old gals drank: Joan Crawford sipped vodka from a flask, while Judy Garland slugged Blue Nun. In fact, we even know what year certain actresses had their plastic surgery. We could chart a star's career not just by her film roles but also by her operations: "Oh yes, that movie was made three years after the eyes were done, but just before the tummy tuck."

To accumulate all this knowledge we had to begin early. As soon as we learned to read, we began studying the stars until our frontal lobes contained more Hollywood bits than an IBM computer. We were like MGM computers. By the time we were teenagers we could spout more trivia than a Universal Studios tour guide. But it wasn't just the major stars who got our attention. Most of us absolutely swooned over the oeuvres of character actresses completely forgotten by the average man on the street. Single-handedly we've kept alive the legends of Eve Arden, Karen Black, and Maria Ouspenskaya. If they ever organized a Zasu Pitts film festival, you'd find crowds of gay men—and only gay men—lining up outside the theater for tickets.

In fact, it was this early recognition of, and continuing appreciation for, the lesser known dames that really was a cornerstone of our budding gay consciousness. Living in the margins, we were more aware of the margins of show business, and we were more appreciative of the great talents who worked hard yet never became really well known. Anyone might watch *The Women* and laugh at that hilarious old dowager spouting lines like, "Bring me a Bromo-Seltzer, and put a little gin in it." But only a gay kid would bother to learn that her name was Mary Boland and that she also did a great job as Mrs. Bennet in *Pride and Prejudice*. Likewise, any straight person could watch *All About Eve, The Misfits,* and *Rear Window* and be floored by Bette Davis, Marilyn Monroe, and Grace Kelly. But only a gay kid would appreciate that the "tough cookie" holding her own with those legends also had a name, and that it was Thelma Ritter.

So when it came time to pay tribute in this book to the great actresses of Hollywood, we decided that the lives and personalities of Bette, Judy, and Marilyn had already been mined more thoroughly than the state of West Virginia, and even second-rate legends like Carol Channing and Lauren Bacall have drag queens imitating their every shimmy, wink, and flutter. We would therefore like to present to you three character actresses who, each in her own way, were fascinating for young gay kids. What distinguishes these three actresses is that each one has come to be recognized as the best exemplar of a specific type. They achieved this distinction by giving at least one fabulous archetypal performance and then going on to give that same performance in every film in which they subsequently appeared.

The Tramp: Dorothy Malone

If there was one character type in movies that fascinated gay boys above all others, it was the sleazy Hollywood bad girl. Knowing that our own sexual natures were taboo, we identified with every peroxide blonde we saw, from Mae West through Madonna. This sultry, tough-talking, fast-living, no-nonsense dame was our first clue that people could survive outside the erotic boundaries epitomized by Ozzie and Harriet Nelson. For gay boys, she was the one face of Eve we most wanted to emulate, and she was easy to spot onscreen because whenever she walked down the street, we'd hear a sultry sax on the soundtrack and cigarette smoke would waft up from the corner of her lips.

To better understand this type, one doesn't have to sit

through a whole slew of bad films. Luckily for us, one screen portrait of a tramp stands out among all the rest, and that is Dorothy Malone's completely over-the-top Academy Award–winning performance in Douglas Sirk's *Written on the Wind*. Ms. Malone's Marylee Hadley, the nymphomaniacal bad sister of Robert Stack, the girl in love with Rock Hudson, was the epitome of pulsating passion, and she served as the unsung role model for all the great trampy performances that followed, from Elizabeth Taylor through Divine.

How did we know that Marylee was a tramp?

First of all, she acted like a tramp. She was always bored and restless. She shimmied her breasts when she danced and when she looked at a man her mouth parted slightly. Secondly, she dressed like a tramp. Dorothy always wore tight, low-cut red dresses, in contrast with her costar, Lauren Bacall, who was costumed conservatively in gray suits. Malone also had dyed blond hair with dark eyebrows. (Her eyebrows were so thick, in fact, that they looked like two little mink stoles, and with Dorothy's convulsive overacting, when she raised one of those babies, she practically threw it over her shoulder.) She also wore too much mascara, another sure sign of trampiness, because according to 1950s morality, when a girl lost control of her eyeliner she'd soon lose control in bed.

Thirdly, everyone *knew* she was a tramp. Her libidinous nature was the topic of much conversation among the other characters. Even her brother called her a "filthy liar" to her face, which she qualified: "No. I'm filthy. Period." In fact, the only character who wasn't absolutely certain she was a slut was her straightlaced father who, when his daughter was denounced by the local gas station attendant, acted shocked, as though it were possible he hadn't been aware that she'd been boffing every man in town.

In the film's most memorable scene, the old man decides to reprimand his daughter and we watch him slowly walking up the long staircase of the family mansion to her room. We then see Marylee in her room, loosening her dress as she listens to wild bongo music. The camera then takes us back to the broken-hearted father, who sadly plods up the stairs. Then back to the daughter, who has slipped into a chiffon negligee and now wiggles her shoulders lasciviously to the music. Then back to the father as he reaches the top of the stairs. Then back to the daughter, who's rubbing a framed photograph of Rock Hudson against her heaving bosom. Then back to the father, who suddenly suffers a stroke. Then back to the daughter, orgasmically kicking her feet in the air. Then finally we watch the father tumbling down the stairs, and one last shot of the wicked daughter laughing maniacally.

By killing off her thick-headed father with loud music and dirty dancing, Dorothy Malone deserves to go down in history as one of the greatest Jezebels of all time. In the suceeding decade Ms. Malone gave us a few more overheated performances—including one as Mia Farrow's mother in the TV version of *Peyton Place*—but none of them could ever equal the dazzling bravura of her Oscar-winning turn. So before we lose this piece of gay film history forever, we'd like to add a new variation to that old slang term for gay, "a friend of Dorothy." From now on we'd like to see every trampy gay man referred to as "a friend of Dorothy Malone's."

The Screaming Victim: Veronica Cartwright

Ever since Fay Wray made a name for herself howling in King Kong's hairy paw, there have been many great Hollywood screamers, but none of them is more deserving of recognition than Veronica Cartwright. It wasn't just her vocal abilities—her thrilling high notes, her whimpering lower register—that put her in the first rank of screamers. It was also the fact that her characters never had a shred of good fortune or human dignity. She was just about the most pathetic, put-upon, and pushed-aside loser to ever suffer a career in Hollywood.

The sister of another

child star—Angela Cartwright—Veronica made her first major screen appearance in Alfred Hitchcock's *The Birds.* In this downbeat flick she played Rod Taylor's younger sister, and we first saw her miserable face when Tippi Hedren arrived in Bodega Bay carrying two caged love birds, which she gave to Veronica as a gift. Luckily for us, Mr. Hitchcock knew a great talent when he saw one, and he gave Ms. Cartwright plenty of opportunity to simper, sob, and become generally hysterical in the face of the mounting bird attacks. Her best moment was when she had to describe what happened to her teacher—the chain-smoking Suzanne Pleshette—in which she sobbed the immortal lines, "Then the birds covered her. Aaaah!" Meanwhile, Jessica Tandy looked horrified as this juvenile stole the picture right out from under her.

Unlike many child stars who couldn't make the transition to adult roles, Veronica was eventually able to leap from girlish crying to womanly wailing. In the 1978 version of *Invasion of the Body Snatchers,* she played Jeff Goldblum's girlfriend, and, if that wasn't horrifying enough, she eventually got the life force sucked out of her by the usually mild-mannered Donald Sutherland. After this rather exhausting experience, Veronica tried to stretch as an actress. In that great sci-fi horror film *Alien,* she held back the howling and gave a subtly agitated and quietly hysterical performance. And, finally, in her most sustained adult role, Veronica achieved her career pinnacle in an otherwise mediocre film by playing a psychotic housewife in *The Witches of Eastwick*—in which she got to projectile vomit cherries all over her living room. She was absolutely brilliant.

In short, we would heartily recommend that any gay boys looking for a career in female impersonation check into the possibility of imitating this unsung heroine of horror. It wouldn't be easy. One would need great vocal fortitude and an equally strong stomach. But the final results would be worth the effort: Veronica Cartwright's career is a life lesson to all of us and should be preserved for posterity. As gay men we should never fail to remind ourselves that, no matter how homophobic society becomes, there have always been people whose problems were much worse than ours—with far more limited resources to handle them.

The Smart Ass: Hayley Mills

Long before Boy George and *Absolutely Fabulous*, there was another British import that completely charmed the gay hearts of America. When straights refer to the sixties British invasion, they are most likely thinking of the Beatles, et al., while for gays the expression is probably an homage to the first time they saw Hayley Mills in *The Parent Trap*. Hayley was different from other child actresses—wise beyond her years and just a little bit of a tart. What made her so intriguing was that, in movie after movie, she never toed the line but always came through a winner. We loved her because she wasn't your typical girl-next-

door, and yet she somehow made it to the top of the Hollywood heap. Even when playing Pollyanna, she was never nauseatingly sweet like her American counterparts, Shirley Temple and Margaret O'Brien.

In Walt Disney's *The Parent Trap*, Hayley played identical twins forced to live apart by divorced parents Brian Keith and Maureen O'Hara. After the girls struggle to reconcile their folks, the movie ends with the parents reunited and the two faces of Hayley Mills living happily under one large suburban roof. Nowadays, this film is fondly remembered for the consummate skill with which Ms. Mills was able to characterize two sisters who looked exactly alike and yet were totally distinct. It was an eerily accomplished performance—not unlike that of Jeremy Irons in *Dead Ringers*. Viewing this movie today is like seeing the reverse effect of Ashley and Kate Olsen on the TV show *Full House*. Back then, we had one talented little girl portraying a set of twins; nowadays we need a pair of untalented twins to portray one little girl.

Hayley Mills's indisputable queer masterpiece, however, was *The Trouble With Angels,* in which she played a rebellious girl in a convent school who holds her own against Rosalind Russell, who had somehow progressed from Auntie Mame to Mother Superior. Hayley, who was then a young teenager and in the twilight of her career, managed to accomplish what most gay boys only dreamed of: She skipped swimming in gym class for four whole years by using preposterous medical excuses. She also smoked in the bathroom, gave the Nazi salute to Ms. Russell behind her back, and uttered the immortal line, "I've just had a *scathingly* brilliant idea!" Then, at the end of the movie, she made the ultimate queer career choice. In the greatest religious miracle since Jennifer Jones saw the Virgin Mary, Hayley Mills gave up the idea of marriage and opted for a life in the nunnery. This was probably the last mainstream movie in which becoming a nun was considered a happy ending, but Hayley was always full of surprises.

Sadly, this supersuccessful child star all but disappeared from the screen afterward, and—like Jane Hudson—she suffered the indignity of eventually being eclipsed by her sister Juliet Mills, who had a TV hit with *Nanny and the Professor.* But for any gay boy who grew up while Hayley's star was burning bright, she was an indelible influence. Independent, loyal, wisecracking, and resourceful, Hayley epitomized the one thing that we queers most look for in a female star—a gay man's sensibility.

THE SUPERSTAR: DORIS DAY

Veronica Cartwright, Dorothy Malone, and Hayley Mills were three actresses who made great contributions to gay life, and yet none of them had long careers as stars of the first rank. On the other hand, there was Doris Day, who, for twenty years, was one of the biggest stars in Hollywood and who from 1962 to 1964 was the number-one box office draw in America. No other actress was so widely popular and yet, strangely, Doris Day is scarcely appreciated nowadays.

If Doris Day is discussed at all, it's for the sex comedies she made with Rock Hudson, starting with *Pillow Talk* in 1959. Unfortunately, in the years that followed, she became stereotyped as an overage virgin, and when the social climate changed radically, she became a cultural dinosaur overnight. In defense of her films, it must be said that Doris was actually a pretty good role model. She usually played independent career women, and she never embarrassed herself by acting desperate or man-hungry. If at times she seemed a little hysterical or uptight, it wasn't from protecting her virginity so much as from preserving her dignity against scripts that were occasionally misogynistic and stupid.

In addition, many gay men—to paraphrase Oscar Levant—knew Doris before she became a virgin. She was, in fact, an incredibly versatile performer. She had a voice like Rosemary Clooney's and a body like Sophia Loren's. She could play comedy as deftly as Shirley MacLaine and melodrama with the skillfully restrained hysteria of Susan Hayward. She was, in fact, a great entertainer and character actress who also happened to be beautiful enough to play leading ladies. In *Love Me or Leave Me,* she was a battered torch singer. In *Midnight Lace,* she was a terrified newlywed. In *Please Don't Eat the Daisies,* she was the loving mother of a large brood. If nothing else, she gave the world "Que Sera Sera," and she even had one truly astounding dyke performance in *Calamity Jane,* in which she sang, "my secret love's no secret anymore." In addition, there was also something gay-friendly in her choice of costars. As she got older she stopped making movies with the likes of Clark Gable and James Cagney and started surrounding herself with closet queers like Rock Hudson and fey supporting players like Paul Lynde, Robert Morse, Terry Thomas, and Tony Randall. For this reason alone, her movies back in the sixties were hugely enjoyable for queer kids, and no superstar gave us more hours of popcorn-munching pleasure.

So why has she been forgotten? In truth, Doris Day made dozens of good films, but not a single great one that would have emblazoned her image in our minds as Judy, Barbra, and Liza have. But, when all is said and done, Doris Day still has her loyal and highly informed fans. We just tend to keep our identities under wraps. Let's face it, if you ever started spouting details about *The Glass Bottom Boat* at a party, you'd probably be labeled as the Man Who Knew Too Much.

Chapter 22

Gays on Film

One obvious reason that actresses were so popular with gay boys was that there weren't any avowedly gay men in films to look up to. Until the seventies the only quasi-queers in cinema were closeted sidekicks like Edward Everett Horton, fussy retail clerks like Franklin Pangborn, and a few scattered tortured souls, psychopaths, and suicide victims. In fact, in his landmark book *The Celluloid Closet*, Vito Russo writes that, "In twenty-two of twenty-eight films . . . from 1962 to 1978 . . . major gay characters on screen ended in suicide and violent death." We believe that there's a very simple explanation for this statistic: If gay characters were killing themselves, it was probably from severe depression over how they were being portrayed in the movies. Let us therefore take a closer look at the various manifestations of this phenomenon.

The tortured soul: The cliché of the masochistic homosexual was popularized by Tennessee Williams in the 1950s. For some reason, Williams made a career out of creating these miserable individuals, even though photographs from this era always showed Williams himself having a pretty good time. If only he'd been able to write a play about his summers in Provincetown, a whole dreary genre might have been avoided. Instead, we had movies like *Cat on a Hot Tin Roof,* at which we wanted to scream, "Brick, leave the South, move to New York, and find a new Big Daddy!" (This also leads us to the question of why so many homosexuals back in the fifties had geological names like Brick and Rock; what, then, does this imply about Fred Flintstone and Barney Rubble?)

A subset of the tortured homosexual was the drunken homosexual. If one were to believe what we saw on the screen, gay men did nothing but drink themselves to death at miserable parties. Two examples from the sixties were *Boys in the Band,* in which the gay men at least had some birthday cake with their cocktails, and *The Killing of Sister George,* in which, along with her booze, one lesbian was asked to drink the other's bath water. All in all, these films were pretty sorry sights, and the most tortured homosexuals of this era were the poor gays in the audience who needed a couple of shots of vodka just to sit through such grim tales.

The psycho queer: Ever since Leopold and Loeb became notorious in the 1920s, straight screenwriters have delighted in creating gay psychopathic killers. One would hope that this stereotype might scare off fag-bashers, when in reality it only seems to perpetuate the myth that gays are a menace to society. In *Psycho,* we had the queer mama's boy who killed a motel patron instead of bringing her fresh towels, forever tarnishing the good names of millions of gay men currently working in service industries. Then, in *Dressed to Kill* and *Silence of the Lambs,* the killers are cross-dressing maniacs, leading one to conclude that tight pumps are one of the prime causes of homicidal rage. Finally, in the James Bond adventure *Diamonds Are Forever*, the evil villains are two gay killers who dress up as—guess what?—waiters. James Bond actually dispatched one of these creeps by torching him, which delighted every member of the audience who'd ever had bad service in a restaurant.

The suicide victim: Once again we might thank Tennessee Williams for establishing this stereotype with *Suddenly Last Summer*. This ludicrous movie was the gory drama of a gay man vacationing in Italy who goaded a group of cannibalistic children into serving him for dinner with a bottle of Chianti. An even more egregious example of this genre, however, was *Ode to Billy Joe*, in which Robby Benson committed career suicide by playing the hypersensitive gay hero. In this movie, Mr. Benson mysteriously jumped off the Tallahatchee Bridge, and the audience was left to wonder: Had he heard Bobbie Gentry drone that depressing theme song just one too many times? Or had he seen the movie *Deliverance* and feared that these were typical gay men in that part of the country? Or maybe Robby had just read the reviews for his most recent film and finally realized that he had about as much charisma as dry toast?

Although during the seventies Hollywood continued to feature psycho queers in such films as *Cruising*, it also made a belated attempt to portray the real lives of some unapologetically post-Stonewall men. Certainly the most glossy of these efforts was the painfully awkward *Making Love*, in which Michael Ontkean and Kate Jackson played a married couple whose idea of a good time was singing Gilbert and Sullivan songs with an elderly neighbor played by Wendy Hiller. Ms. Jackson—who'd been so clever in *Charlie's Angels*—didn't seem to have a clue that a man who sang operetta could possibly be gay. In the climactic scene, when her husband informed her that he'd been sleeping with Harry Hamlin, she responded by dropping a casserole dish on the linoleum, at which point her concerned husband jumped up immediately, not to comfort her but to wipe up the mess and repolish the floors.

In the eighties we saw the beginnings of a new trend, the gay next-door neighbor who drops by a woman's apartment, delivers a punch line and some comfort, and then leaves—almost as if the sexuality of the characters typically played by Tony Randall was finally being acknowledged. Unfortunately, the actors in two of these roles, Nathan Lane in *Frankie and Johnny* and George Carlin in *The Prince of Tides*, were directed to mince so outrageously that the resultant performances were among the least subtle portrayals of minorities since the days of Amos and Andy.

In the nineties, *Philadelphia* has achieved success by casting established stars in a movie about a gay man suffering from AIDS. Unfortunately the screenwriter didn't seem to think that audiences would identify with the gay protagonist, played by Tom Hanks, so he wrote the story from the point of view of Denzel Washington's character, an uptight straight man, creating a weird hybrid of a movie, not unlike *An Early Frost* wrapped in an earnest episode of *Home Improvement*. Most recently, *Interview With a Vampire*, from a book which tried to parallel sleeping in a casket with coming out of a closet, grossed over a hundred million dollars, and many industry watchers are interpreting this as a sign that the American public is now ready for mature gay subject matter. On the contrary, this film did little more than repeat the idea that homosexuality is only acceptable among monsters who prey on one another and lurk in the shadows, which is hardly a message worth sending out to gay children.

Chapter 23

Home Movies

We couldn't end this section on gay cinema without writing about those wonderful home movies our fathers made of us back in the fifties and sixties. Watching them as adults, we're amazed that our dads might have believed, even for a moment, that their baby boys were straight. The evidence is incontrovertible, because in those early years before we learned to rein in our natural impulses, we unselfconsciously entertained our relatives, flouncing around the yard in our grandmothers' sunhats and making hand gestures that even Liberace would avoid.

And it's not as though these films were easy to make. In those primitive, pre-camcorder times the making of home movies was grueling, backbreaking work. At every birthday party Dad would set up more lights in our den than were at a night game at Yankee stadium, laboriously screw the camera onto its tripod, and then order us to open and re-open our presents until the shot was perfect. Those darn lights, hot enough to grill chicken breasts, so blinded us that our retinas would shrink to the size of neutrons, making it impossible to distinguish a pair of socks from a necktie. Meanwhile our guests' ice cream cones were quickly melting from the heat, and our mothers were becoming anxious suburban Stella Adlers, coaching our performances from the side. But we gladly endured these inconveniences, because we loved those subsequent family screenings at which we would get into our pajamas, eat Cracker Jack, and stay up way past our bedtime. First our mothers would complain bitterly about their weight and Dad would have to reassure them that the apparent size of their thighs was the result of poor camera angles. Then our fathers would play the film backward and we would howl from seeing ourselves blowing out birthday candles and then, in the next instant, sucking them back on again.

Seen today, these films are very revealing of the strange symbiosis between fathers and gay sons: In a rare confluence of interests, their need to be Erich Von Stroheim perfectly matched our need to be Gloria Swanson. For the only time in our lives, we were actually encouraged to camp it up, because the more outrageously we mugged for the camera the better was the quality of Dad's film. Unfortunately, the only thing missing from these movies are more scenes of the old man himself. Ironically, as he invariably worked the camera, he was rarely a part of the scene, and if not for our memories we might watch these movies today and imagine ourselves as fatherless back then as those poor little March girls in *Little Women*.

Enslaved by the Bell:
Adolescence and Beyond

Part Four

"By evening I had settled any doubts I still had about
who I wanted to invite to the prom. And so, with sweaty palms
and butterflies in my stomach, I finally asked Paul."

—Aaron Fricke, high school student who had to sue his principal
to be able to bring a male date to the prom in 1981.

Chapter 24

High School

Most any gay man would rather be forced to sit through a Vanilla Ice film festival than have to go back to being a teenager. Adolescence was supposedly the happiest time of our lives, and yet the very word can still cause us to wake up screaming in the middle of the night. Humiliating memories from these years are still so painful that many of us later attempt to let go of the past by seeking out such seminars as "forgiveness workshops." One of our friends informed us that he recently attended a "healing" weekend, in which his group had been instructed to bring photographs of people who had annoyed or bothered them in their youths. They were then told to throw the pictures into a pink heart-shaped garbage pail. Our friend, without hesitation, flung away his entire high school yearbook.

One of the reasons high school may have been so miserable for us was that we completely lacked role models. In retrospect, we were anything but unique: We'd undoubtedly been surrounded by queers without knowing it. Though we didn't realize it back then, the assistant principal was probably dressing up on weekends as Jane Russell and the social studies chairman was probably cruising the bus drivers. But instead of openly gay teachers, our high school years were often dominated by grim homophobes like our drivers' ed instructor, invariably some retired colonel who usually taught his course with all the charm of a field officer invading North Korea, and who assumed that, just because we were males, we would automatically understand what he was talking about. Many of us knew nothing about cars, so when he asked if our automobile at home had a "clutch" in it, we sometimes responded, "No, but our mother has a lovely handbag." Even more embarrassing was when he ordered us to "Check the mirror!" and we pulled the rear-view mirror toward our faces and examined ourselves for unsightly blemishes.

Even more depressing was the school's guidance counselor. Most of these individuals combined the sullen bureaucratic sensibility of workers at the Department of Motor Vehicles with the intellectual acuity of toll booth employees. They were usually dour chain smokers who couldn't wait to get rid of students so they could run to the faculty lounge for their next cigarette. They were at a loss as to how to advise us; the first question they typically asked in our annual sessions was something like, "What do you want to do when you get older?" And we would look at them in their stuffy cubicles, imagine ourselves in their position, and think to ourselves, *"Jump out a window."*

Let's face it, these counselors weren't Ann Landers: Their advice was worthless, and they looked as if they needed our help more than we needed theirs. The only way they prepared us for our futures as gay men was to show us what it would be like to be stuck at a cocktail party with a boring know-it-all. As far as career advice, they usually knew nothing about us except what was contained in some cardboard folder, and so they generally pushed us in completely predictable directions. If we weren't particularly bookish, our destiny was some sort of vocational program in which boys automatically become auto mechanics and girls dental technicians. At the very least, guidance counselors were unprepared for any uniquely talented students. Our guess is that if Superboy had gone to a counselor for career advice, he probably would have been discouraged from developing his superheroic gifts, and instead he would have been told to do something practical with his heat vision, like keeping fries warm at McDonald's.

Sometimes, in an effort to help students who were unsure of themselves, guidance counselors offered us "aptitude tests." These examinations often put the gay students at a disadvantage, because many of us will pursue careers that aren't presented as options. It's unlikely, for instance, that RuPaul was ever told in high school to sing pop music dressed as a woman. And if the aptitude test told us we were a "people" person, it didn't mean that we should be imitating Barbra Streisand in some smoky cabaret. And, finally, as far as using guidance counselors to talk to about our sexuality: Forget it! One look at these guys and we learned a valuable lesson—being gay was something we'd have to figure out for ourselves.

In retrospect, wouldn't it have been great to have had one unapologetically queer drama coach to help us get our bearings? Then we might have had such items in the yearbook as: "Mr. Tuttle, the faculty adviser for the piano bar club, had a banner year with his highly acclaimed production, the all-male version of *L'il Abner*." And if some gay shop teacher had burst out of the closet, he might actually have taught us something useful—like how to shop. This guy would have lectured us truthfully: "Oh, honey, don't bother making your mom some cheap-looking ashtray. Buy one at Fortunoffs!!" And a gay health teacher might have inspired safer driving by showing us Hollywood movies featuring stars who had died in auto accidents. There would have been nothing like a Jayne Mansfield film festival to make us keep our heads behind the wheel.

Some of us were lucky enough to go to private schools in

which flamboyant queer teachers were more in evidence—and some of us even attended high schools for the performing arts, through whose portals no straight teacher had ever passed. These latter institutions were generally much more fun, as we were prepared for careers in show business by learning how to act, sing, dance, and sometimes even wait on tables in the school cafeteria. When attendance was taken, rather than saying "present," we were more likely to sing a rousing chorus of Sondheim's "I'm Still Here!" The one problem with performing arts schools was that their academic programs were at times notoriously inadequate. A friend of ours who attended one such school recently admitted that everything he knew about World War II he'd learned from *The Sound of Music.* He was actually shocked when we told him that Dwight D. Eisenhower—and not Julie Andrews—was the person most responsible for defeating the Nazis.

GAY MATH

One way in which we might have learned some useful information about being gay was through math problems using actual situations from the lives of gays and lesbians. Why not try to answer some of these problems yourself? Don't forget to show all calculations in the margins. The answers, by the way, are not in the back of this or any other book.

1. Two young professional drag queens start preparing at 10:00 A.M. for an 11:00 P.M. performance that night in the East Village. Miss Brenda is carefully applying eyelashes one at a time, while Cerise Sorbet is painstakingly sewing rhinestones onto her brassiere. At the show that evening they both will earn approximately six dollars each. How long before they both go back to school to study computer graphics?

2. A million and a half gay men and lesbians go to Washington to march for their civil rights. The National Park Service regularly underestimates the number of participants by counting only one out of nine who exit from the Port-o-sans. What was their estimate for the size of the crowd?

EXTRA CREDIT: How long do you think this nonsense can continue?

3. A "Christian psychiatrist" recently started a communal home for gay men who wanted to be turned straight. The men all shared the household chores. Determine the amount of time (in microseconds) it took for one of these clients to begin hallucinating that he was Liza Minnelli taking out the garbage at the Betty Ford Clinic.

4. *La Cage aux Folles* opened on Broadway in 1982 and ran for five years. It was not only a strong statement for gay rights but also a sterling opportunity for leading men to rejuvenate their sagging careers by portraying aged homosexuals. The male lead was played at different times by Gene Barry, Peter Marshall, and Van Johnson, for an average run of eleven months each. At this rate, how long would the show have had to run before the producers offered the part to:

1. Karl Malden
2. Ernest Borgnine
3. Jack Palance

5. *Honcho* costs $4.95 in the U.S. and $5.95 in Canada. The Canadian dollar is worth 83 cents. Therefore, if you were driving to Toronto from New York, how much money could you save by buying the magazine in Buffalo?

6. Margaret came out to her parents as a lesbian in 1978. Her parents made her see a psychiatrist for forty weeks at sixty-five dollars a visit. How many Melissa Etheridge albums might Margaret have bought with the money they could have saved?

7. Light travels at the speed of 186,000 miles per second. Unflattering light seems to travel twice as fast. How long before a typical gay man demands that they remove the ugly fluorescent bulb from above his desk at the office?

8. After a man copulates with a woman, the sperm impregnates the egg in approximately four minutes. How many lifetimes before this information is actually useful to you?

GLAMOUR GRAMMAR

Another way young gay men might have been helped in high school would have been by being taught their mother tongue—gay English. As we mentioned in an earlier chapter, gay men have their own peculiar grammar, which differs from standard usage in several ways. The most obvious element is the common use of the third-person pronoun "she" when referring to either gender. The purpose of this tradition is to blur the hard distinction between the sexes, which has made patriarchal culture so unfestive throughout the ages.

Some gay men are so steeped in this practice that masculine pronouns have all but disappeared from their vocabularies. Also, in many cases, the more overtly masculine the subject, the more adamant the speaker is about using the feminine pronoun. The following examples are actual snippets of overheard conversations:

1. "My father? Oh, she's retired now."

2. "Bryant Gumbel? I'm so over her!!"

3. "Richard Nixon? She was an evil woman."

4. "Arnold Schwarzenegger? She's a big girl, all right."

Another interesting facet of gay grammar is its tendency to take certain feminine proper names and to use them as all-purpose labels. The most popular example of this is "Mary." Whereas "Mary" is commonly used to denote a particular female, many gays use "Mary" to classify any member of an entire category of men. In other words, in a room containing 200 gay men, you could easily have 200 Mary's.

Two slightly less common examples of this phenomenon are the words "Carol Ann" and "Theresa." These terms serve a similar function to the ubiquitous "Mary," but they tend to be used in more specific circumstances. "Carol Ann," for instance, generally refers to a gay man from the Midwest who has moved to New York and is now trying to break into show business, such as in the sentence: "Is that big Carol Ann doing another cabaret show?"

"Theresa," on the other hand, generally refers to a gay person of the Catholic persuasion, especially one in a high clerical position.

(Note: In a similar vein, some gay men like to avoid the suffix "man" and use "woman" instead. "A Walkman" becomes "a Walkwoman" and David Letterman can be rechristened David Letterwoman.)

In many other cases, gay men simply take standard grammar and refashion it to suit their own particular needs. Following are but a few examples:

1. The gay accusative tense: "What's her problem?"

2. The gay subjunctive: "If only I were in a hit Broadway show I could quit catering for good."

3. The gay conditional: "I'd date him if he asked me."

4. The gay hair conditional: "I'd date him if his roots weren't showing."

5. The correct gay propositional phrase: "You come here often?"

6. The incorrect gay propositional phrase: "You want to go see a movie starring Mel Gibson? He's my favorite actor!"

7. The gay direct sex object: "I would definitely like to kiss Frank."

8. The gay indirect sex object: "I would definitely like it if Frank kissed me."

9. The gay past tense is something that happened in the past, such as in the sentence: "Johnny went to the supermarket."

The gay past progressive tense is something that happened in the past and continues into the present, such as in the sentence: "Johnny has been going to the supermarket."

The gay past perfect tense is something that occurred in the past and—if life were perfect—it never would have happened, such as in the sentence: "Johnny went to the supermarket, met some hunk at the deli counter, and I haven't seen him since."

10. And, finally, the one singular sensational tense. This is the verb tense used to describe any gay man who is, was, or ever will be in the cast of *A Chorus Line.*

Chapter 25

The Totally Ridiculous Homosexual History of the United States of America

or, Above the Fruited Plains

Many gays loved history when we were kids—where else could we get rewarded for knowing gossip? Unfortunately, history was written by the victors, so we gays have never been accurately represented in school texts. As far as the real lives of Socrates, Alexander the Great, and Michaelangelo are concerned, historians have adopted the policy, "Don't ask. Don't tell." Therefore, by the time we got to high school our interest in history had most likely waned considerably. It all began to read to us like the story of many poor guys dying in wars fought for homophobic religions or lands where you wouldn't want to live anyway. The typical straight hero was just some bloated monarch with seven wives who, without a crown on his head, couldn't have gotten a date for Saturday night. As far as we were concerned, the Ottoman Empire might as well have been a country filled with footstools. Where were the queers? How was it possible that we were taught American history, for instance, without one mention of homosexuality? So in order to redress this imbalance, we offer, for your enjoyment, the following timeline. (We may have exaggerated a little . . .)

1492 From the very beginning gay men are quite active in searching for new worlds. In fact, when Columbus returns from his first voyage, several gay men protest, "Oh, he didn't discover America! We were there last weekend. It's not that great."

1621 The Pilgrims land first on the site of what is now Provincetown, Massachusetts. They see a few topless lesbians on Herring Cove and get right back on the boat.

1650 Puritanical Cotton Mather tries to suppress homosexuality. Meanwhile his gay cousin 100% Cotton Mather invents the stocks (for recreational purposes). The following year straight people decide to use it as a form of punishment.

1692 The Salem witch trials put a real damper on Halloween parties. Gays are targeted. In a shocking development, a drag queen is thrown into prison for dressing up as Elizabeth Montgomery and uttering those famous lines, "Mother, you take that spell off Darren right this instant." Her accuser is her nosy next-door neighbor, Hester Kravitz.

1765 The British institute the infamous Stamp Act, in which gay and lesbian bar patrons must now pay a cover at bars and taverns and have their hands stamped.

1776 Betsy Ross sews the first American flag. Ms. Ross is helped by her two backup sewers, Florence Ballard and Mary Wilson, who are later pushed aside when Betsy claws her way to the top.

1814 Francis Scott Key writes our national anthem, which is first sung publicly by that perennially troubled singer, Connie Francis Scott Key.

1825 The Marilyn Monroe Doctrine states that foreign powers should keep their female impersonators out of the Western Hemisphere.

1862 Civil War! In one of the bloodiest battles of the war, General Stonewall Jackson leads his troops of cross-dressing rebels in handbag to handbag combat.

1871 Gay men move West looking for real estate bargains.

1876 Alexander Graham Bell invents the telephone. His first words to Mr. Watson are, "What are you wearing?" Mr. Watson replies, "A lab coat, sir."

1881 Thomas Alva Edison invents the light bulb, and within hours his gay nephew, John Michael Edison, invents the dimmer switch.

1903 Wilbur and Orville Wright make their first airplane flight at Kitty Hawk. Their younger gay brother, John Michael Wright, goes along as the world's first flight attendant and serves his brothers honey-roasted peanuts.

1905 African-American inventor, John Michael Washington Carver, discovers over 300 uses for peanuts, including Thai noodles with a spicy peanut sauce.

1927 The first sound film. For the first time we can hear the voices of Hollywood stars, a great boon to drag queens who had been unsuccessfully trying to lipsynch to Louise Brooks.

Chapter 26

How to Be a Sissy in Gym Class

By far the most humiliating high school experience for every gay man was gym class. God. How we dreaded this hour! Our major source of discomfort, of course, was the gym teacher himself. If we were lucky, he was a handsome hunk, invariably newly wed, getting his degree in "leisure studies" from a local community college. But far more prevalent was the broken-down ex-wrestler with enough curly hair on his back that he could easily be mistaken for an air conditioner filter. This guy was typically such an animal that he could have shaved first period and still managed to grow a full beard by the end of the day.

Gym teachers made a lot of noise. They yelled a lot to inspire enthusiasm in their pupils. They generally barked clichés like, "Losing is not in my vocabulary!!" (This seemed obvious to us, because the typical gym teacher always looked about 150 pounds overweight.) It should be further noted that his bark was often worse than his bite. Most of these men didn't enter their professions in order to work hard, and thus a carefully

planned program of passive resistance wore them out sooner
than we expected. Therefore, as the first step in letting him
know that we weren't the enthusiastic type, we learned how to
stand like sissies. Now, the archetypal sissy-
in-gym class position had three basic com-
ponents. As we describe this stance, you
can practice in the privacy of your home.
First, get up and place your legs about
three feet apart. Then:

1. Drop all your weight to one
side and let your arms hang
languidly at your sides. This
action immediately creates a deli-
cious sense of stasis and relaxation.
Now, imagine that there are bullies
on either side of you who for no
reason whatsoever would like to
kick the crap out of you.

2. Grab your arm behind your back.
In this position you are jutting out
your stomach, immobilizing your
limbs, and thus making the statement
to the world that you are totally useless. You are now far less likely to
be picked for any team
and much more likely to
have a ball thrown at your head.

3. Stare at your fingernails. We mean *really* stare at them,
with fingers splayed and upturned. This activity creates a
sense of narcissistic completion and total alienation, thus

further enhancing your rather casual attitude to whatever is happening around you. You now may also judge appropriately whether or not a manicure is in order. When we were in gym class we also quickly learned that the most appropriate facial expression for this stance was staring straight ahead, pursing our lips, and letting our eyes go blank. Under no circumstances did we make eye contact with anyone else in the room. And if we had to look at anything other than our own navels, we only lifted our eyes mournfully in the direction of the clock.

Because gym class was such a traumatic experience, we've decided to investigate this subject in greater depth by dividing it into specific activities, from the least to the most heinous:

1. Volleyball. There were certain team sports in which it was fairly easy to get lost in the crowd. Volleyball, if played correctly, was merely an exercise in standing around and doing nothing. We had only to assume the basic pose as described above and hope to stay out of the way. The trick in volleyball was to position ourselves next to the tallest, most hyperactive team player we could find. Thus, whenever the ball came anywhere near our vicinity, this gorilla would leap in front of us and send the ball flying back from whence it came. Every now and then, we might have glanced upward as the ball sailed over our heads. Our teammates certainly appreciated this modicum of interest vis-à-vis the outcome of the game. We then went back to contemplating our cuticles.

Note: Every now and then the gym teacher might yell "Rotate." Please restrain yourself from doing a pirouette!

2. Football. This was another team sport in which it was fairly easy to not do anything. Better still, it was played outdoors, where we could get some fresh air while avoiding interaction with the other players. Best of all was that thrilling moment when all the other boys got in a line and bent over. At this point, avoiding the temptation to stare, we joined the line with our teammates and imitated them as best we could.

One of our fellow players would inevitably yell "Hike," at which point we would start running. It wasn't important that we knew where we were going, just as long as we looked somewhat determined. It was highly unlikely that the quarterback would throw us the ball, but if he did, we ducked, because if we caught it, we would then be the object of much unwanted attention from the other team. Once again, as with volleyball, the trick was to stay as close as possible to some gorilla who would reach out and catch any projectiles thrown in our direction— and if our gym teacher tried to counter our plan by yelling "Stay open! Stay open!" we just didn't listen to him. After all, we weren't the Seven Eleven.

3. *Basketball*. This game was made tricky by the rule that, for some obscure reason, we weren't allowed to carry the ball as we ran down the court. If we forgot this rule and instinctively tucked the ball under our arms like a clutch, some thug would yell at us, "Don't travel with the ball." The best response to this would have been, "The next time I go to Florida I'll leave it home!"

4. *The President's Physical Fitness Test*. This was the day when most of us would rather have been deported than show up in class, for our gym teacher now began to ask us to do things like climb up one of several fifty-foot ropes. Considering the physical conditions of several of our recent presidents, we are astounded that this ritual is still being foisted upon our youth. Reagan's physical fitness test might have been finding his bifocals, while Clinton's might consist of hoisting a Big Mac to his mouth.

5. Wrestling. This sport prepared many young gay men for adult life. For one thing, it was the first time that we had to choose whether we wanted to be a "top" or a "bottom." It was also the first time we lied about our weight, because the smaller we were, the smaller our opponent was. As a means of learning self-defense, however, high school wrestling was next to useless: Any moves we learned were applicable only if we just happened to be on our hands and knees and our assailant just happened to be grabbing our elbow. So unless we habitually ride the subway in this position, we should probably study another form of self-protection.

6. Dodge ball. We hesitate to even call this activity a sport; we'd rather think of it as God's plan for kids with no future to get their revenge on National Merit Scholarship winners. To excel at dodge ball one needed only a good throwing arm and a complete lack of human kindness. If sports were meant to build character, then dodge ball was designed for boys with psychotic episodes who needed creative outlets. This game could well have been invented by South American generals to torture political prisoners, and every time we played we considered applying to Amnesty International to set us free. The only sure way of getting released from this torment was by immediately throwing ourselves in front of the ball and getting disqualified from playing any further. Once safely on the sidelines, we could give the finger to the opposing team.

7. Baseball. Baseball was the worst, and so we've saved it for last. Let's face it—some of us were so bad at throwing baseballs that even our dogs wouldn't play with us. To make matters worse, it was the one sport most often foisted on us by otherwise uninterested fathers. One queer we know was actually given a baseball by his dad and told that he should go get it autographed. Our friend immediately took the train to Times Square and had it signed by the original cast of *Damn Yankees*.

Now, in baseball we couldn't get lost in the crowd. Rather, our team captain would give us a position, and we would then be expected to do something. Of course, maximum creativity was required to find a place where we would do the least damage. Fortunately, some positions required less participation than others, so we were usually stationed in right field. If a lefty came up to bat, however, we were suddenly shifted to left field. If he could switch hit, then we were moved to second base, unless, of course, there was already a man on first, in which case they put us on third base. If the bases were loaded, however, our team captain simply slipped us a bus ticket to Poughkeepsie and shouted, "Get the hell out of here!"

Once again, we had to be aware of certain lingo. If we were told to "cover" right field, we had to resist the urge to go out and buy linoleum. Rather, this meant it was time to skip merrily to our place in the sun, assume an appropriate pose, and begin praying that the ball wouldn't be hit anywhere near our vicinity. We generally distanced ourselves as far as we could from the batter—the next county, if possible—because it was always easier to run forward, then run back for a ball that had gone sailing over our heads. And if by some catastrophe the ball landed anywhere near us, we didn't even attempt to throw it into the infield. We knew we threw "like a girl," and rather than heave the damn thing, we just ran the ball to the infield, asking plaintively, "Who gets this?" Eventually somebody took it from us and did whatever he had to do.

At some point, when the inning was over—no thanks to us—

our team got its chance at bat. In many cases the team that was forced to take us also got a favorable handicap, so we were never surprised when our side was allowed five outs, or the first baseman on the other team was forced to play blindfolded. While waiting for our turn to strike out, we relaxed in the dugout and tried not to speak to our teammates. We were also especially careful not to be hit by the baseball, which could have been the result of either a wild pitch or our gym teacher's venting his frustration. When we actually did get up to bat, the other team's outfield often took our appearance as an opportunity to catch up on their sleep. Although we had been given instructions about what to do if we hit the ball, we never bothered to learn them, as this happened infrequently. Rather, if by some miracle, our bat so much as touched the ball, we merely waited to hear the impassioned screams of "Run, you idiot!" and dutifully scampered wherever we were told to go.

In conclusion . . .

Gym class is an experience we never forget and—in all fairness—if gay men aren't welcome in the military, then neither should we be forced to take gym class. Ironically enough, most gay men do wind up becoming fitness freaks as they get older and stay in shape far longer than most straights. Apparently, we queers take quite naturally to exercising once the threat of humiliation is removed. After all, when was the last time we had to worry at a health club that we'd be the last one picked by a personal trainer?

Chapter 27

The Boys in
the School Band

A Seattle-area high school recently tried to ban gay kids from becoming members of the student council. What a joke! We say, why not just ban gay kids from all school activities? The fact is, we gay kids have always been the backbones of many student organizations. Who do they think put the glee in glee club? Without gay kids there would have been no yearbook, no girls' athletics, and whom would they have gotten to star in *Anything Goes*? You might say that before we moved downtown and became club kids, we'd already been club kids back in high school. For one thing, these school organizations were great channels for all of our repressed hormonal drives. If we couldn't kiss the object of our unrequited love, at least we could put our tongue to use licking envelopes to raise money for our school band. In addition, high school clubs were an easy way to gain a measure of acceptance: There were no prohibitive cover charges or velvet ropes back then. Also, unlike the case of sports teams, we didn't have to try to belong: We needed only to show up at the appointed hour, and we were in.

And then there was also that unspoken hope, a repressed genetic drive, that if we joined enough clubs we might connect with members of our own tribe. Safety was in numbers, and sure enough, many of those kids with similar interests turned out to be closet queers just like ourselves. This reason alone was good enough to endure the often dreary routine of late afternoon club hopping, which meant staying after school five days a week, walking to some dingy classroom, waiting an hour for everyone else to show up, arguing for five minutes about whether or not to have a bake sale, and then running out just in time to catch the late bus home. This isn't to say that we were totally indiscriminate in our choices of extracurricular activities. As with TV and films, clubs could be labeled Queer and Non-Queer.

Queer Clubs

The yearbook: It was, ironically, we gays who assembled the high school yearbooks, often with the bizarre notion that we would someday want to remember what was for some of us the most miserable four years of our lives. We were the writers and the editors who had no lives of our own because we were so busy documenting the activities of everyone else in school. We were also the school photographers, those lonely guys who worked overtime trying to make the cinderblock facades of our school buildings look artistic. We also specialized in photographing the sun rising over parking lots and dreary mood shots of lockers.

As we thumb through our yearbooks as adults, we marvel at the hokiness of these art shots, along with the candid photos of cheerleaders wolfing down meatloaf sandwiches, as well as those dark, slightly unfocused snapshots from theater productions, which always caught the leading man in the most effeminate poses imaginable, leading us to wonder whether Mary Martin had been in our graduating class. Finally we would be thrilled by those action shots of some varsity pole vaulter sailing magnificently over the seventeen-foot marker, closely followed by a group portrait of the Future Nurses Club valiantly trying to help this young man regain the use of his limbs.

Then, as we continue to peruse the class photos, we laugh riotously at the other kids' misshapen faces until we get to our own picture. None of us looked eighteen; we all appeared to be either seven or forty-seven. And what were we wearing? No matter what year we graduated from high school, it was always a transitional period, some time between the heyday of the beehive and the dawn of stringy hair parted down the middle. And was there ever a time when plaid hip huggers were in style, or were they just taken out of mothballs once a year to be worn for class photos? And why, after wearing perfectly decent clothes all year round, would we suddenly want to look as if we'd just returned from a yard sale at Neil Diamond's house?

Drama club: One of those perennial chicken-egg questions has always been "Are gay men attracted to the theater because they're inherently theatrical, or do gays become theatrical in order to go into the theater and be surrounded by other gays?" We tend to believe that we're congenitally expressive and that drama club merely gave us the wonderful opportunity to do in public what we'd been doing in private all our lives, and garner a much different response. In other words, if we wailed "Everything's Up-to-Date in Kansas City" on our mother's coffee table, it brought a far different reaction than doing it on the stage of a five-hundred-seat auditorium. It may also be that gay men are more theatrical than straights because we're not afraid to pirouette to the beat of a different drummer. After all, if we're heading toward a lifetime of performing socially unsanctioned sex acts, we're not likely to worry about having our masculinity questioned for dancing down a staircase in *Hello Dolly*.

Then again, gay men may simply be more talented than straights. Recent studies suggest that the two halves of the brain, the sensitive and the analytic, get along fairly well in gay men, whereas in straight men the two halves have chosen to ignore each other completely, and, in more extreme cases, bicker constantly. In other words, the rational side of a straight man's brain is often found bashing the artistic side, which then finds it hard to be creative while cowering in a corner of the skull after years of relentless abuse. We don't wish to imply that straight men never indulge in the performing arts. There is, in fact, a club almost completely filled with heterosexual theater lovers; it's called Stage Crew.

Musical clubs: Then there was the school orchestra which, when it wasn't playing bad music, was usually selling candy bars in order to raise money to go out of town. Most of the school would gladly have supported our travels if only for the reassurance that we would never return. A close cousin to the school orchestra was the school marching band, consisting of a group of nerdy musicians who deluded ourselves into thinking we were jocks because we played our music while marching up and down the football field. If we were the rare gay man with no musical talent, the band director could usually find us an instrument, even if it was only a triangle.

But the greatest haven for marginally talented gay men was the school choir. This was the group that performed its overlong holiday program every December, mixing show tunes with Christmas carols and at least one Chanukah song, even if the closest Jew was more than three counties away. The tragedy of school choirs was that they gave many of us the mistaken notion that we could sing, though in reality we were simply being drowned out by the forty baritones behind us. How many of us later moved to New York after graduation to seek careers in show business, plopped down two months' rent on a studio apartment, and were told at our first auditions that we were completely tone deaf?

Creative writing clubs: Every high school had a literary magazine invariably called something like The Flame, because most of the poetry therein deserved to be torched. This group generally gave us the chance to be big fishes in small ponds, because most of these cadres had no more than three core members. In addition to us aspiring Allen Ginsbergs and Gertrude Steins, there was usually one morose Sylvia Plath wannabe who wrote poems about how she'd someday climb into the oven and stab herself with the meat thermometer, as well as one painfully thin, long-haired lyricist who would spend the next fifteen years of his life working in Tower Records while trying to form a rock band in his parents' basement.

Language clubs: For gay kids, foreign languages were always fascinating, as they always held out the possibility that we might someday get to live anywhere other than where we were brought up. For those of us too shy to open our mouths in downtown Des Moines, the dream that we might one day be chattering up a storm five thousand miles away on the Champs Elysées kept us enrolling in French classes two years after every straight boy had dropped out. How we queer boys, and only we queer boys, loved this most romantic of all the Romance tongues, the language of Molière, Voltaire, and Jean Paul Belmondo! In fact, we would guess that there hasn't been a straight man fluent in French on this side of the Atlantic since Lafayette's last tour of America in 1824.

Now, the purpose of the French club was to augment the academic program by giving us firsthand experience of French culture. Unfortunately, it was often impossible on our limited budgets to do much more than eat French fries, make French toast, and watch Mr. French on TV. Meanwhile, in other parts of the building, the Spanish club was watching *El Cid* for the fourteenth time, the Russian club was eating fried blinis, and the German club was organizing its annual Beer Hall Putsch and making secret plans to march into the Polish club.

Service organizations: A lot of gay boys grew up as Momma's boys and later evolved into people pleasers and teachers' pets. In high school we were invariably drawn to service organizations like the PA Announcement Staff, the Cafeteria Workers, and Student Office Help. These were nothing more than excuses to use students without paying the minimum wage. Many of us queers were thus duped into doing jobs that should have been done by the slothful and exploitative staff of the school. Thus librarians were able to thumb through old issues of *Redbook* while we were reorganizing their shelves, and kitchen workers were able to smoke out back and eat pizza while we were slaving over their steam tables. The original idea of joining these organizations was that they would somehow look good on our records, as though an Ivy League school would be impressed that we knew how to use an industrial floor polisher. Or else we were told that these skills would be useful in the real world, for instance, operating a mimeograph machine—a technology that was outmoded thirty years before we got to high school.

Political organizations: The Student Council was another organization that frequently attracted gay kids, if only because it gave us budding members of Queer Nation our first opportunity to wrangle concessions out of thick-headed bureaucracies.

And, of course, any gay students interested in politics were probably also members of the debating team. Unfortunately, these debates were usually on topics in which most of us had no interest. Should Red China be admitted to the UN? Ho-hum. If only the gay students had risen up and argued for truly fascinating topics we might have seen the following: "Jim Nabors—Why should anyone care?" or "The drapes in the auditorium—Is there any excuse for them?"

Non-Queer Clubs

Career clubs: And then there were clubs we rarely joined, such as Future Accountants of America, which presupposed that we gay boys were on some kind of predictable career path. These organizations could rarely hold our interest because, as a rule, gay men go through careers faster than Madonna goes through friends. Who could have predicted in high school that we'd later become a gynecologist, a set designer, and a forest ranger all in one lifetime? If we'd been true to our feelings, we would have had to attend a different career club every day of the month. In addition, many of the careers we imagined were hardly fodder for high school clubs. What would a meeting of the Future Go-Go Boys have looked like? Would we have arranged the school desks to form a runway in the middle of the room and stripped down to our G-strings? And what would the future Flight Attendants of America have done during a club meeting? Pointed at the exits and smiled?

Rifle clubs: There were some clubs in high school that no self-respecting queer would join. Chief among these were groups like the Sharpshooters, in which pasty-faced psychopaths were always pictured in the yearbook as scowling at the camera with their guns aimed at the photographer. Why schools encouraged these activities was beyond us. And where did these clubs meet? On the roofs of school buildings, along with their sniper scopes? Even more troubling was the idea that the parents of these kids naively believed that these were benign activities. For every rifle club member was there a helpful mother in the background, dutifully rinsing out a ski mask in Woolite and packing lunches for those seven-hour sieges?

Science clubs: The classic nerd groups. Most of us avoided such organizations because, being queer, we had enough problems without having to defend our membership in the geology club. These were the kids who would spend their entire academic careers working on a science fair project, like demonstrating nuclear fusion in an old Maxwell House Coffee can. Science clubs were valuable, however, in that they gave more reserved students a sense of inclusion and a feeling of power. From our experience, however, they should have been more carefully monitored. Who knew that the moody foreign-exchange student—the one who never missed meetings of both the rifle club and the chemistry club—would one day leave his bookbag behind in drivers' ed, resulting in a car bomb explosion when a cheerleader hit a speed bump?

Sports: There were gay men who played football and lacrosse, but for the most part we gravitated toward sports that emphasized individual achievement, such as track. Then for those of us with absolutely no athletic ambitions, there was always the Bowling Club, a form of exercise only marginally better aerobically than being trapped in an iron lung. Most of the time we sat around waiting for our turn, and by the time we actually got our thirty seconds on the alley, we'd already burned off more calories by pulling levers on the vending machines.

THE BRAVEST KID IN SCHOOL

There was always one kid in high school so effeminate that any attempt to hide his gayness would have been absolutely futile: He was the first out gay person that any of us knew. We all recognized this kid immediately. He was the guy with the turned-up collar carrying a curling iron in his shoulder bag; he was the guy not afraid to hang half-naked posters of Shaun Cassidy inside his hall locker; he was the guy sitting at the back of the room, legs crossed, sharpening his pencil with an emery board. In short, he was the one gay man who knew from the start that he was destined to be a flight attendant, a hairdresser, or a decorator—or, as he would announce: "Air! Hair! or Flair!" On his aptitude test, he would score highest in attitude. And though we often feared for his life, his openness was often his strength, because for every queer who was beat up by the jocks, there was another queer who could turn his effeminacy into a bargaining chip. He would do this by shamelessly becoming the confidant of the prettiest girls in school. This way, if any jock wanted to get laid that year, he'd have to tiptoe around this guy or suffer malicious gossip. In conclusion, we can only say that we never had the nerve to befriend this character, and yet we've never forgotten him, either.

Chapter 28

Great Expectations: Gay Boys and the Opposite Sex

There's a common misconception that gay men don't like women. Nothing could be further from the truth. As kids, we often found girls much more congenial and compassionate than boys—they were quicker to get our jokes, and we shared many common interests. It was only when the pressure began mounting to date girls that our problems with the opposite sex really began. Initially, we gay kids tried to maintain an innocent attitude—it was everyone else who suddenly started acting strange. Every time we hung out with Debbie and read her *Seventeen* magazines, our mothers got all excited and began planning our weddings. Then whenever we spent the day with Melanie listening to the B-52s and singing along with Belinda Carlisle, the other guys started getting jealous and calling us a "lady's man."

By junior high school, it was the straight guys who were going through the major changes, not us. They were the ones leering at the centerfolds while we were still reading *Playboy* for the cartoons. They were the ones who started talking "dirty" about girls while we were just shaking our heads and pretending to keep up. Desperately, we tried not to look dumb, but inevitably we would feel left out. One of our friends told us that his older brother got suspicious one day and snapped at him, "I bet you don't even know what hooters are. Go ahead. Use the word 'hooter' in a sentence!"—at which point our friend blurted out defensively, "Hoo-ter hell decorated this room?!"

When we got to high school, the pressure to be macho intensified. All of a sudden, the girls with whom we'd been hanging out started going through their own mysterious changes, clustering together and telling secrets among themselves. It was as if they expected us to play a game when we didn't know the rules and weren't sure what the prize was. Gone forever was the casualness of intergender friendships. And—to add insult to injury—we learned that if we wanted to be real men, we would have to pay for the privilege by taking girls to the movies and picking up the entire tab. Suddenly, we realized why the straight boys all were worrying about money and getting part-time jobs. Heterosexuality, besides feeling unnatural, seemed awfully expensive.

So, there we were, being pulled in two different directions. On the one hand, we were suffering peer pressure to date women. On the other hand, we were feeling queer pressure just to be ourselves. Often we were simply confused, and it didn't help us that society offered little in the way of support. Even so-called experts were giving advice that—in retrospect—was pretty absurd. We know one gay man who claimed that he didn't realize that he was gay because he'd read a column by Dr. Joyce Brothers stating that it was perfectly "normal" for straight men to have fantasies about other men. We can only guess what Dr. Brothers would have written if she'd known that our friend's fantasies involved bodybuilders on Fire Island with exquisite taste and wicked senses of humor.

So for all the above reasons, many of us simply surrendered to the inevitable and went through a period of dating women in high school. Quite frankly, not all these dates were hideously painful. Some of them were quite pleasant, especially when we got to gossip about TV shows and which other boys we thought were cute. But, of course, there were always those awkward moments when we were at the movies with our arm around Susan, while we were getting aroused by John Travolta up on the screen. And there were those *really* awkward moments when we brought the girl home and we were expected to show a little passion out there on the stoop.

As the game grew more difficult to play, we developed several strategies for avoiding sex with girls altogether:

1. We dated girls who seemed as if they might be frigid, or at least afraid of the very idea of sex. The worst part of this strategy was that it was unintentionally cruel to the girls; it can be traumatic for a straight woman to date a gay man because then she might go through life expecting all men to really listen to her. These girls weren't too hard to spot. They generally wore sweaters even on hot spring days, or they sat by themselves in the cafeteria and never looked boys straight in the eye. Such neurotic young women were often perfect for queer boys, because they elicited a compassion from us that often made us forget our own little secrets.

2. We dated girls with high moral standards. These were the young women who went to Catholic high schools carrying Mother Teresa lunch boxes. For best results, you could cruise the advanced catechism class, but Mormons, highly orthodox Jewish, and Shiite Muslim girls also fell into this category. The important thing was to find a girl who would appreciate it when you told her that you would never take advantage of her before marriage. And if you could find a girl who wanted to be "respected" even after marriage, that was even better.

3. We dated girls who were highly protected. The best thing to do was find a girl who had a Sicilian father who would threaten to kill us if we deflowered his daughter. This way we had the perfect excuse not to smooch. The best part was getting to bargain with the father. If he demanded that we bring Maria home by eleven, we would tell him that we'd get Maria back by 10:30, and not a minute later! If he then compromised and said 10:45, we would say, "Deal!" And if we brought her back a second later than 10:45, we smacked our fist on the table and demanded to never see his daughter again.

THE PROM

Why was prom night such a nightmare? For many of us, it was the difficulty in finding a date. Since we probably weren't as courageous as Aaron Fricke, one of the first students in America to bring his boyfriend, our prom date was usually a girl from one of the above-mentioned categories. Then there were those of us who had made every effort to avoid our own prom but were later roped into it by some gal who had just broken off with her steady and needed an escort.

In any case, this was the usual order of events: To start with, we had to rent a tuxedo for the first time in our lives, so the rental companies foisted on us all those garish outfits that no self-respecting adult would have worn. We usually wound up in powder blue or maroon, with a hideously ruffled shirt and a bow tie the size of an eggplant. Even more disappointing was going to the florist, where it seemed awfully unfair that our date should get an orchid while we only got a wilted carnation for our buttonhole. But on this and all other matters of protocol, we dutifully listened to the advice of our elders and, in due time, we felt so beaten down we could have been sold a funeral horseshoe wreath read-

ing "With deepest sympathies from the Mosconi family," and we wouldn't have known the difference.

Worst of all was the endless picture-taking as we left the house, as though our parents had to capture a lifetime record of heterosexuality in only fifteen minutes. Meanwhile, we wanted to scream at them, "Take as many snapshots of me as you can, because this will be the absolute last chance you'll ever get to see me with a girl!" The prom dinner itself was generally prime rib, steamed broccoli, and a baked potato that had been in the oven since 1954. Some of us had our proms in catering halls, while many of us suffered the indignity of passing the night in a school gym which had been pathetically festooned, as though green crepe paper hanging from the basketball hoops would make us feel like we were in Tahiti.

When the band began playing, we danced to everything from "Daytripper" to Meat Loaf's "Bat Out of Hell." The musical high point was generally a Motown medley in which thirty-seven songs were mercilessly ground down into the exact same tempo. By eleven o'clock—as other couples went behind the gym to make out—we would have to make up some excuse about a cold sore breaking through our skin. At eleven-thirty we'd bring our date home, which meant that, by midnight we could go back to our houses and revert to being gay pumpkins. The following morning we'd nonchalantly come down to breakfast while our folks waited expectantly for a progress report. But we had nothing to say. Our brief, shining moment of heterosexuality, like the orchid corsage, had already wilted, and no amount of refrigeration could maintain it one second longer than necessary.

Chapter 29

Bone-anza
or The Gay Boy Surviving Puberty

G oing through puberty isn't easy for anyone. Puberty, in fact, is torture, a hazing ritual from God. All of a sudden we have more hormones shooting through our bodies than a Montana cattle ranch, and we find ourselves aching to do things we couldn't have imagined the week before. Our comfortable, self-contained world of childhood is blown to smithereens. Puberty is when you go to the beach, see a lifeguard, and, suddenly, more than anything else in the world, you want to be rescued—from your family.

Gay teenagers are generally even more confused about the feelings that have suddenly dropped into their laps. We had no guidance, and no role models. For one thing, we didn't know how to find other gay teenagers and, back then before MTV and ABC Afterschool Specials, there certainly weren't any gay teenagers being portrayed on television. Just as alienating was the fact that the straight teenagers on television were being portrayed by the likes of Henry Winkler, who could only have been a good role model for other thirty-five-year-old actors.

Therefore, our first crush was often on some unknowing straight guy who was inadvertently torturing us by taking off his shirt on a hot summer day. This experience often led to years of frustration, because for some reason, straight guys have always been notoriously reluctant to date other men. It's no wonder that so many gay men excel in creative fields: Our imaginations are unusually well developed from all our teenage fantasies. In fact, if the heart muscle could have been built up like biceps from resistance, then most of us would have had upper bodies more pumped up than that of Mr. Olympia. While our straight peers were going out on dates and trying to get to first base, we were still free agents, willing to play, but unable to find our team.

So for years we wandered through the minefield of unrequited passions, our insides as shattered as Dresden after the fire-bombing. Some of us were captivated by the rebels and the bad boys. Like Madonna, many of us couldn't resist the twisted sneer that we knew masked a boyish vulnerability. When the school bully barked at us to meet him after school, we seriously considered going there with a box of flowers and some chocolates. Then there were the newly hired janitors, the young ones whose uniforms always managed to stay pressed and unstained. When they drove around the playing fields on their lawn mowers we dreamed of hitching a ride. Then there were the college guys who made extra money selling ice cream in the neighborhood. How many of us gained twenty pounds and got aroused every time we heard the Mister Softee theme song? Or how about that unmarried third cousin on your mother's side, the one who wasn't really related to us by blood, the one who kept sitting next to us at family functions and stared at us every time we went to the Viennese table for another cannoli?

These were the guys who absolutely slayed us. We're not talking puppy love—we're talking pit bulls chomping away at our solar plexuses. And our crushes were completely unpredictable. We liked them old. We liked them young. We liked them sweet. We liked them mean. When we were younger, our types were as unique to us as our fingerprints, and yet we authors have managed to come up with three major categories of crush material—the types we *all* fell for.

1. *The boy next door.* This was our first crush—the baby crush. What made this boy so attractive was that he was simply the first male we laid eyes on after we went through our changes. One day we were kids together building go-carts and gluing model airplanes; the next day everything was different.

- We asked him to give us rides on the back of his banana seat so we could have an excuse to hold onto his thighs.
- When we played hide and seek, we looked only for him.
- We sat at our window with binoculars waiting for him to come back from Little League.
- We knew when he was going to take a shower, so we rushed over to his house with a dry towel.
- We befriended his mother, hoping she would invite us to stay to dinner.
- We bought a tent and suggested sleeping out in the backyard.
- If he wanted to play guns, we became the army doctor.
- We started inventing new games like Strip Monopoly.
- We badgered our parents into buying a pool, because we knew how much he liked to play submarine attack.
- We offered to rub suntan lotion on his back—in December.
- We gave each other massive wedgies. He thought it was a practical joke. We thought it was true love.

- If he was having trouble with his long division, we offered to do his homework for him—for the rest of his life.
- We tried to sit next to him in Holy Communion class— and we were Jewish!

2. *The most perfect boy in the school.* A few years later we had bigger fish to fry. We were now in high school, suffering a totally anonymous crush on some guy from the other side of town. This was the guy we had to love from afar. He was the most handsome. The most popular. The best dressed. He was in all the honors classes, but he was also the captain of the lacrosse team. Even the principal of the school genuflected when this young god walked by so:

- We ran three miles out of our way just to be at his bus stop, from which we then took the bus one mile to school.
- We memorized his class schedule, and then scampered to wherever he was so that we could then stroll behind him to his next class.
- We always sat directly behind him in algebra class because his butt looked so cute when it stuck out through the back of his chair.
- In gym class we wanted to lie about our weight so we might actually get to wrestle with him, and we were in heaven when he pinned us to the mat.
- At football practice we positioned ourselves to be tackled by him and him alone.
- We dreamed of bringing a loofah with us into the school shower and offering to scrub his back.
- Every time we masturbated we were tempted to send him flowers.

- In total desperation, we wanted to hire the school bully to beat up his girlfriend.
- At the end of four years, we wanted to sign his yearbook, but we knew we'd be writing steadily through August if we put down our true feelings.

3. *The most attractive teacher in the school.* There was always one. He was the ex-football star who came back to his hometown to teach American history. He was the sensitive English teacher who was the student adviser for the school literary magazine. He was the painfully shy chemistry teacher who wielded a Bunsen burner like nobody else. He was the man we wanted to be. He was the only one in the world who would understand our secret wishes and desires. In short, he was the first man in the world on whom hairy legs looked attractive so:

- We found his convertible in the parking lot and slowly ran our fingers across the vinyl slipcovers.
- We wanted to take algebra five periods a day—four years in a row.
- We bought wing-tipped shoes, just like his.
- We found ourselves writing sonnets.
- We wept through repeated viewings of *To Sir with Love*.
- We found ourselves humming the theme song "To Sir with Love" twenty-four hours a day.
- In chemistry lab we tried to re-create his scent.
- At lunchtime we fantasized about bringing romantic candles to the faculty lounge and asking the cafeteria lady to dim the lights.

One of the reasons that high-school crushes were so difficult was that gay boys and straight boys often had the problem of getting aroused in the most inconvenient places. So from the earliest age, we gay boys learned to control ourselves by closing our eyes and thinking about Aunt Sylvia—or trigonometry—or Aunt Sylvia doing trigonometry. We became experts at self-discipline, which is why so many of us were amused at the weird argument that we gay men wouldn't have been able to control our sexual desires if we were allowed into the military: Any gay man can tell you that we've been controlling ourselves for years. But for those of us who had a little trouble with our eyes wandering in the gym-class shower, we simply could have stopped bathing altogether and smelled like a pair of dirty socks for four years, or we could have found the homeliest boy around and placed this troll between us and the really cute ones.

Or in the unlikely event we did find ourselves with an unwanted woody, the best defense would have been a big whopping lie:

- Look at that! It must have swelled up from that soccer injury!!
- Oh, look! How convenient! A towel rack to hang my wash cloth on!
- It's hereditary. My mother has the same problem when she showers.
- It's a chia penis. Just add water and . . .
- You think this is a hard-on? Nah! It's always this big!

Chapter 30

Sticks and Stones

The most harmful F word in the English language doesn't have four letters—it has three, and it's spelled F-A-G. Nothing hurts a gay kid more than being insulted by homophobes. A friend of ours recently told us how he'd been outed in Catholic elementary school. His accuser was his sixth-grade teacher—a nun—who, one day had the nerve to tell this little boy in front of the whole class, "You act just like a girl!" Our friend was mortified and took the next day off from school. When he returned the following day, the nun demanded to know where he'd been. This little boy looked his teacher right in the eyes and said, "Woman's problems!"

What made these attacks so frightening was that our tormentors actually believed they had the *right* to ridicule us because they were backed up by "traditional values." But the truth is that homophobia has always been a refuge for cowards. That foul-mouthed gonzo in the shower who was the most afraid about dropping the soap was usually some slob who never even used the soap to begin with.

Which didn't make the taunts any less upsetting. If anyone called us a "faggot" our first impulse was to pretend we didn't hear anything. Our second impulse was to pray that the word "faggot" had been used only in the general sense of "dork, nerd, or asshole," because almost any of these insults would have been less harmful than the truth. Is it any wonder that certain words filled us with dread, like "cocksucker"? We hated this word—even though we were being accused of something we hadn't ever experienced. The worst, though, was "homo." H-O-M-O. There was no defense against this insult, which inexorably unveiled the truth. These four letters were so frightening that many of us developed lactose intolerance just from seeing them on the sides of milk cartons.

The complete word "homosexual," on the other hand, sounded vaguely scientific, so we would sneak into the library to look it up in some dusty old medical dictionary. This was an incredibly stressful experience. Our worse nightmare was that we'd find the word and next to it instead of a definition we would read: "WHY ARE YOU LOOKING UP THIS WORD?!! WHAT'S WRONG WITH YOU?!! DO YOUR PARENTS KNOW THAT YOU'RE HERE?!!" At which point an alarm would go off, and everyone we knew would suddenly appear out of nowhere, fully aware of what we'd been doing.

Our only solace at this time came from unusual sources. We were devoted followers of Ann Landers's column, because she could generally be relied upon to express the point of view that "God's creatures come in all sizes and shapes." Or else, there might have been some somber afterschool special, or a transvestite character on an episode of *Quincy*. But we never let on that we had a secret area of concern, and while watching television with our family, if the word "gay" was mentioned, we'd automatically stop breathing. When the programs were baseball games, we had to be careful that nobody knew what a turn on it was when their uniforms were tight. On the other hand, when we watched the Miss America pageant, we tried not to let on that we liked the talent portion of the show best of all. And that we loved the Miss Universe pageant, not because the contestants were sexy but because they paraded around in those hilarious costumes of their native lands. The trick was to be absolutely silent at all times, even when we most wanted to scream with laughter.

In short, we became experts at surviving in hostile environments. For the gay kid, the world of heterosexuals was like a jungle with predators lurking behind every tree, and like all natural prey we adapted strategies for distracting our enemies and avoiding any direct confrontations. As avid watchers of the Discovery Channel we authors now believe that not only is homosexuality natural, but the solutions we found to protect ourselves from attack are also part and parcel of—

The Wilde Kingdom

1. We developed thick skins. There are many creatures, such as the tortoise, who lumber along carrying their shells on their backs into which they can retreat at the first sign of danger. Similarly, many gay kids simply developed natural armor and learned not to care when they were verbally abused. Another version of this behavior was for a kid to appear so distant and vague that the other kids hardly noticed him. This strategy of subterfuge was probably our major line of defense. The problems came later on in life when we wanted to get closer to people and we were still lugging around more baggage than Elizabeth Taylor on her way to the airport.

2. We became even more flamboyant. There are other animals who develop bizarre mannerisms to spook their enemies, such as lizards who have oversized flaps and can turn their faces inside out. In the world of the gay teenager, we could see this type of behavior in the boys who hid their sexual orientation behind a show of colorful eccentricity. This was the kid who wore chartreuse sneakers, shaved a third of his head, and wore his mother's blouses buttoned up the back. These "weird kids" generally short-circuited the bullies who would have insulted them had they only known where to begin. These were also the kids who, years later, made millions designing frocks for anorexic women and mincing for the camera on the *Fashion File.*

3. We kept moving. Then there are the roadrunners. Many gay kids protected themselves in high school by maintaining such a breathless pace that nobody could catch them. They participated in every extracurricular activity imaginable in order to avoid having to leave the safety of the school grounds. They edited the yearbook, starred in the class show, played on the tennis team, soloed in the woodwind section, and organized the prom committee. They even made up a few clubs of their own—the Future Card Shop Owners of America. In answer to the question Why are so many gay men so talented and versatile?, one answer could be: It was better than getting the crap kicked out of us after school.

4. We were bitchy. In contrast to those who chose flight over fight, were the scorpions, the porcupines, and the killer bees, who were just so prickly and full of comic zingers that taking them on was hardly worth the retorts. These were the highly courageous "snap queens" whose hauteur was unshakable and whose wit never failed them. These were the "sissies" who would look the bullies right in the face and snarl in a sour soprano, "Got a problem? Take a picture. It lasts longer." In later life, these kids generally found employment in the burgeoning gossip industry or, if they lived in small towns, wrote scathing critiques of community theater.

5. *We infiltrated the enemy.* And, finally, there are the animals who protect themselves through camouflage, such as the king snake, which has the ability to pass as a poisonous coral in order to avoid being bitten. The gay version of this mutable reptile was the guy who wore all the trappings of the ruling clique—the penny loafers, the varsity sweaters, the creased khakis—and would say or do anything to fit in, even if it meant selling other gays and lesbians down the river. We authors can forgive this self-protective sneakiness in frightened teenagers, but we find this behavior totally reprehensible once this type has been elected to Congress or has ascended to the executive offices of a major Hollywood studio.

To one degree or another, we all learned how to hide. We hid what we knew. We hid who we liked. We learned not to display our fingers when we looked at our nails but rather to bend our fingers toward us. We learned not to let our hands bend backward at the wrist. We learned not to be too fussy with our clothes, and we even mastered the art of carrying our schoolbooks under our arms, even though clutching them against our chests would have been much more comfortable, and carrying them in a totebag would have been the most fun of all.

But mostly we learned to keep our mouths shut, knowing that sooner or later we'd get our revenge. And for many of us, this usually came at the twentieth high school reunion, when we saw that the jocks who had tortured us were now three-hundred-pound poster boys for high cholesterol. Apparently, their physiques had the shelf life of sour cream, while we gays usually had managed to keep our youthful figures and look even better than we did in high school. And for some of us justice took a literary form for, as they say, writing well is the best revenge.

HOMOSEXUAL TENDENCIES

It was during adolescence that we first may have heard ourselves described as having "homosexual tendencies." Even back then we knew that this was ridiculous, because, in fact, we didn't just *tend* in that direction, we'd already crossed the border and covered a few hundred miles. And just what were homosexual tendencies, anyway? Would it have been the desire to join a gym at the age of four? Was it an urge to go to Washington, DC, every few years and hold mass demonstrations?

This phrase, "homosexual tendencies," is just one of many such terms that seeks to diminish a primal urge by turning it into a primal whim. In short, it's an insult. A lot of modest biographers will use this misleading term to supposedly protect their subjects. Eleanor Roosevelt, for instance, kept a gal pal in the White House and wrote her passionate and explicit love notes. To describe her as having "homosexual tendencies" would be like saying Henry VIII had "heterosexual tendencies." Which leads us to wonder, what would heterosexual tendencies be? The desire to organize religions and complain about taxes?

There were several other well-meaning yet ultimately harmful phrases. "It's just a phase" gave us the mistaken notion that homosexuality was like acne and would eventually go away. Other misinformed mainstream experts were calling homosexuality a "lifestyle," as though it were something we giddily took up in our leisure time, like roller skating or hang gliding. The most common misnomer, however, was that gayness was somehow a "choice," as though every teenager was given a menu at the age of twelve from which he selected "homosexuality" as a main course, along with large helpings of alienation and abuse on the side.

In short, we never had "tendencies" to be homosexual. We may have been closeted or confused, but hardly any of us were tentative or noncommittal. Our sexual identity did not grow slowly over time like a houseplant tending toward the light; rather we were pretty well set from the beginning. If we tended toward anything, it was that as we got older we got stronger and more independent, and we started defining ourselves in our own terms, rather than in the misinformed language of our childhoods.

Epilogue

The Second
Coming Out

Many of us felt it was a huge relief to finally tell our parents we were gay, because we no longer needed to hide our feelings—about their furniture. But it took years of vacillating to get to that point. Very few of us came out all at once. We were like groundhogs—we'd take a few steps out of the closet, we wouldn't like what we were wearing, so we'd run back inside.

Even if we were anxious to meet other gays, we were confused, because the gay subculture was hidden from view. The only queer establishment in town was some dingy bar on the other side of the tracks with black windows and a neon martini glass on the door. These places, we later learned, were purposely left tacky so straight people wouldn't know that we were there. Unfortunately, this veil of secrecy had also left us in the dark. Therefore, in order to shed a little light for future generations, we would now like to trace the coming-out process, which we see as occurring in four stages:

1. Inside out. When we were "inside out," we were out—but only on the inside. This was a difficult stage. For some of us it lasted a few days, while for others it lasted a few lifetimes. When we were inside out we had some vague idea that we were gay—but then we would suddenly go into denial, at which point we went to great lengths to keep the truth from ourselves. When we were inside out we were prone to many ridiculous scenarios. We sought security in the fact that we fantasized about women, when all we were doing was wondering what the movie *Gypsy* would have been like with Ethel Merman playing the lead instead of Rosalind Russell. It was also during this period that we kept pictures of musclemen on the refrigerator, as a supposed reminder that we were on a diet. If we said we were bisexual—which we said often—the truth was that we liked being both a top and a bottom. What was sad about all this was that we weren't fooling anyone: It just made other people think we were being even more erratic than usual.

This was when we thought that nobody at work knew we were gay, when in fact our sexual orientation was being thoroughly discussed around the water cooler. Whole seminars were being held on the subject, including charts and graphs. We needed to get a grip. If we had a signed picture of Julie Harris on our desk, nobody believed we were dating her. And it was usually those of us who toiled in the gayest industries—like fashion and theater administration—who were the most adamant about our privacy. One guy we know was afraid to come out at work until we pointed out to him, "But, Chad, you write for the *Advocate!*" This was also when we had the hardest time explaining where we'd gone on vacation. If we'd been to Provincetown, for instance, we might have admitted to Cape Cod.

Throughout this phase we remained estranged from our parents, fearful that the news of our being gay would kill them. Ha! If they survived the Great Depression, World War II, and the conformist fifties, it was highly unlikely that any news from us was going to do them in. Meanwhile, some of our parents were already telling their friends behind our backs, "I just wish he'd come out already! All of our friends with gay children get to go to parades and commitment ceremonies. We feel left out."

2. Peeking out. At some point in our lives we started telling people we were gay. Unfortunately, there are no set rules for when this event should take place. Unlike the ritual Bar Mitzvah or confirmation, the timing is best left up to the individual. All we know is that many of us reached a point of complete frustration when we finally challenged God to strike us dead if there was anything wrong with homosexuality. If afterward there were no major changes in the weather, we started yakking away to anyone who would listen. It was at this point that we usually discovered something truly amazing: For years we'd been afraid that nobody would like us because we were homosexual, when in fact it was quite possible to be unpopular for reasons completely unrelated to our sexuality.

The first bridge we most often had to cross was telling our parents, but before we did so we had to find out what they already knew about "gayness." If, for instance, we told our mothers that we'd just come back from the Spike and they replied, "Oh? I didn't realize that the hardware store was open so late on Saturday night,"—then we definitely had our work cut out for us. If, on the other hand, they exclaimed, "They let you in wearing that faggy shirt?", then we knew they were much more informed than we had thought.

Very often, rather than telling our parents, it was easier to practice on less intimidating family members, like our sisters. Most often these sympathetic sisters would then encourage us to tell our mothers, or sometimes they would helpfully do the job for us, usually during their next squabble with Mom. However our parents learned the truth it was usually a great relief for everyone involved. This is not to say that we didn't encounter difficulties: Some parents preferred to go on hoping that their pansy of a son was actually only a late bloomer. Their strategies of denial were limitless. One father claimed to have completely accepted his son's homosexuality, in a long letter written on a *Playboy* centerfold. In general, future research on this subject will show that there are basically three stages of acceptance that all parents go through when a beloved son reveals that he is gay:

1. They don't want to talk about it.
2. They want to talk about it.
3. They want to talk about it on *Oprah*.

3. *Out in the open.* In this phase, we started to relax about our sexuality—as did our parents. Once they adjusted, they very often wanted to show their support by sending us many magazine articles about being gay. We got articles about gays in the military. Gays on Wall Street. Gays in Hollywood. Some parents sent us so much mail on this subject that they could have been arrested for distributing adult literature across state lines. Finally, we began to plead with them to send us clippings on subjects we knew nothing about—like auto mechanics or financial planning. Some of us even got so tired of this barrage of clippings that we went tit for tat, and we started sending them articles from *Modern Maturity* about aging parents who annoy their children.

We also started looking for other members of the family to whom we could come out. One of our friends remembers telling his grandmother, whose response was incredulous. "But how could you be gay? You have that poster of Farrah Fawcett in your room. Those long legs. Those luscious lips!" To which our friend replied, "But don't you remember, Grandma? *You* gave me that poster." But the best thing about this period was that we finally began to understand that we could be happy as gay people. We realized that being gay didn't mean we had to be tortured. And then we started going to the gym, working out, and torturing ourselves.

4. *Out to Lunch.* In our final stage of self-acceptance, we started getting so gay that we began to be annoying—even to other gay people. We felt flamboyant and unconstrained by society. We changed our names just for the hell of it—often taking stage names like Troy—even if we worked in a bank. We joined any gay group that would have us. We even started new organizations, such as Parents, Friends, Casual Acquaintances & Virtual Strangers of Gays. Meanwhile, our parents often joined us in being out to lunch, and some of them were even more political than we were. They drove us to demonstrations, saved us places on floats, and even sewed us costumes to wear at Gay Pride parades. It was during this period that many of our mothers actually gave up needlepoint and started embroidering leather harnesses instead.

And what happened after we were "out to lunch"? Well, eventually most of us just settled down and put things in perspective. We began enjoying the fact that there were gay cruises. Gay bowling leagues. Gay real estate agents. Gay comedians. And often we looked back with just a little regret that we'd gone so many years in the closet. No matter how old we were when we came out, we always asked ourselves why we'd waited so long. Why had we waited so long to accept ourselves? Why had we waited so long to begin dating and learning the romantic skills we should have learned when we were sixteen? And then we realized that no matter when we came out, it couldn't have happened any sooner. Without education there was no way we could have seen where we were going. Coming out had been like putting together a jigsaw puzzle without having the picture on the outside of the box to guide us along.

Then, eventually, most of us decided that, in the final analysis, what blew up our skirts wasn't all that big of a deal morally—but it *was* a huge deal politically. We discovered that we'd become part of a larger struggle because in this era an essentially human function—how one achieves sexual and emotional fulfillment—has been blown way out of proportion.

Merely by accepting that we are queer at this point in history, we have somehow implicitly volunteered for active service in the battle for our country's future, and now many of us are working the battle lines in a civil rights struggle that looks increasingly tense.

So—in conclusion—if there's anyone out there wondering whether or not to come out of the closet, we say, Come out as far as you can. You'd be doing everyone a huge favor. Simply speaking, straight society will never know anything about gays unless we teach it to them. So if we value their education, we owe them the gift of our honesty. Also, coming out of the closet is a gift to ourselves. It's the last step in our maturation as a gay child, because from this point on our lives are completely transformed. It's like putting on a new pair of glasses—not so much virtual reality as getting real. Our incubation period is over and our gay childhoods can finally be seen for what they really were—the prologue for the wonderful drama of being a gay adult. We are now "grown-up gay"—which is when the fun really begins . . . and the subject of our next book.

Author Biographies

JAFFE COHEN has the distinction of being the first openly gay male comic to perform on network television in the United States. After his initial appearance on Fox Television's *Comic Strip Live*, he went on to perform on *StandUp Spotlight*, *Real Personal*, and *The Howard Stern Show*, among others. Cohen's plays *Elliot of Arabia* and *Elliot Bound* were produced at New York's New Vic Theatre, and his one-man show, *My Life as a Christian* premiered at the Courtyard Theatre. His essays have appeared in the *New York Native*, *Outweek*, *QW*, *10 Percent*, and the *Harvard Gay and Lesbian Review*. For film, Cohen wrote and starred in *Chicken of the Sea*.

DANNY MCWILLIAMS is a native New Yorker who began performing stand-up in 1980 at various downtown clubs and cabarets. He also founded and appeared with various comedy troupes, including Premises, Premises which had a lengthy run at The Village Gate. Recently Danny has been criss-crossing the country performing his one-man show, *Twelve Angry Women*, a comic compilation of original characters culled from his experiences growing up in Ozone Park, Queens.

BOB SMITH started doing stand-up in Buffalo, New York, before moving to New York City, where he performed in clubs like The Comic Strip, Catch a Rising Star, and The Improvisation. Smith has been a performer and the head writer for Comedy Central's *Out There*, and worked on a screenplay about a gay stand-up comic for Steven Spielberg's company Amblin. Recently, Smith became the first openly gay stand-up comic to appear on *The Tonight Show* and have his own HBO Comedy Half-Hour. He currently writes a humor column for *Men's Style* and is writing a screenplay about a gay son in a Mafia family.

Since 1988 FUNNY GAY MALES has been the most successful openly gay comedy collective in the world. After an unprecedented two-year run at The Duplex in New York City, FGM went on to strings of sold-out performances in Provincetown, Boston, Philadelphia, Baltimore, San Francisco, Los Angeles, Key West, Toronto, and Sidney, Australia. They have won a Bistro Award from *Backstage* magazine as well as three awards from the Manhattan Association of Cabarets. In 1991, they made history by being the first out comics to be invited to perform at the prestigious Just for Laughs Festival in Montreal. In 1993, they hosted an evening of gay comedy as part of Alan King's first Toyota Comedy Festival in New York City as well as performing for over a million people during the historic March on Washington. On television, you may have seen them on *The Joan Rivers Show*, or *For Comics Only*, or heard them doing numerous stints on Howard Stern's morning radio program.